GW00417546

Governance and Policy in Ireland

Governance and Policy in Ireland

Essays in honour of Miriam Hederman O'Brien

Edited by

Donal de Buitleir and Frances Ruane

First published in 2003
by the Institute of Public Administration
57–61 Lansdowne Road
Dublin 4
Ireland

www.ipa.ie

ISBN 1 902448 97 9

British Library cataloguing-in-publication data
A catalogue record for this book is available
from the British Library

Cover design by Creative Inputs, Dublin
Typeset in Garamond 11/12.5 by Carole Lynch, Dublin
Printed by ColourBooks Ltd, Dublin

Contents

Acknowledgements

The editors would like to thank the authors who responded so generously to their invitation to contribute to this volume. They are also grateful to the Institute of Public Administration and Tony McNamara, Executive Director (Publications) for his assistance in publishing this book. We are also grateful to Eleanor Ashe who acted as copy editor and Hannah Ryan for her help in producing the book.

Notes on Authors

Ruth Barrington is Chief Executive of the Health Research Board, a post she has held since September 1998. Dr Barrington is a graduate of University College Dublin, the College of Europe in Belgium and the London School of Economics from where she was awarded a PhD. She is the author of *Health, Medicine and Politics in Ireland, 1900-1970* (1987), which analyses the forces that have shaped the Irish health services. She has published a number of articles on health and research policy, the most recent being 'Terrible Beauty or Celtic Mouse – the Research Agenda in Ireland' in *New Hibernia Review*, Autumn 2002.

Donal de Buitleir is a General Manager in AIB Group. He was Secretary to the Commission on Taxation 1980-1985 and a member of the Barrington Committee on Local Government Re-organisation and Reform (1990). He was Chairman of both the Advisory Committee on Third Level Student Support (1993) and the Review Committee on Post-Secondary Education & Training Places (1999). He was also Chairman of Comhairle (2000-2002) and of the Lord Mayor's Commission on the Funding of Dublin City Council (2002). He studied at University College Dublin, by which he was awarded a PhD in 1980.

Peter Cassells is a former General Secretary of the Irish Congress of Trade Unions who, from 1987, played a lead role in the development of successive national social partnership programmes. He is now Executive Chairperson of the National Centre for Partnership and Performance. He is also Chairman of Forfás and a Director of the Digital Media Hub. He studied at the Institute of Public Administration and holds honorary doctorates from the National University of Ireland and the Dublin Institute of Technology.

Pat Cox MEP is President of the European Parliament. He is a graduate of Trinity College Dublin. He has lectured in economics at the University of Limerick, and worked as a television current affairs reporter, presenter and investigative journalist. He was General Secretary of the Progressive Democrats on their foundation in 1985, was elected to the European Parliament in 1989 and became President of the European Liberal Democrat Group in 1998. He was elected to Dáil Éireann in 1992 and was elected President of the European Parliament in 2002.

Peter Feeney is Head of Public Affairs Policy in RTÉ. In this capacity he is the designated Freedom of Information Officer for RTÉ. He also acts as Secretary to RTÉ's Election and Referenda Steering Groups and to RTÉ's Executive Board. He was the Editor of Current Affairs Television from 1990-1997. He has a BA in History and Politics from University College Dublin and an MA in Politics from Durham University. Before joining RTÉ he lectured in Politics at the University of Ulster.

Paul Haran is Secretary-General of the Department of Enterprise, Trade and Employment. He holds a BSc (Computer Science) degree and an MSc (Public Sector Analysis) from Trinity College Dublin. In 1989 he was appointed as the Special Advisor to the Minister for Industry and Commerce. He became a Special Advisor to the Chairman of the Revenue Commissioners in 1993 and was appointed as Head of the Economic Policy and Corporate Services Division in the Department of Enterprise and Employment in 1994. He is a Member of the National Economic and Social Council and a Board Member of Forfás.

John Kay is a Fellow of St John's College Oxford and Visiting Professor at the London School of Economics. He has been Director of the Institute for Fiscal Studies, Chairman of London Economics, a director of several public companies and has held chairs at the London Business School and Oxford University. A graduate of the University of Edinburgh, who studied also at Nuffield College Oxford, he is a frequent writer, lecturer and broadcaster, and contributes a fortnightly column to the *Financial Times*. His latest book is *The Truth about Markets,* which was published in May 2003.

Dermot Keogh is Professor of History and Head of Department at University College Cork. A graduate of UCD, he was awarded his doctorate at the European University Institute, Florence. He has published on Irish, European and Latin American church-state relations, on religion and society and on minorities in Ireland. His most recent book, *Jews in Twentieth Century Ireland*, was awarded the James E. Donnelly Sr Prize by the Irish Conference on Irish Studies. He is a member of the Royal Irish Academy and a former senior fellow at the Institute of Irish Studies, Queen's University. He has been a Fulbright Professor and a Woodrow Wilson Fellow, in Washington DC, on two occasions. He is currently completing a biography of Jack Lynch.

Sir Brian Kerr was appointed a judge of the High Court in Northern Ireland in March 1993 and has been in charge of judicial review since 1995. He was educated at St Colman's College, Newry, Queen's University Belfast and Gray's Inn, London. He was called to the Bar of Northern Ireland in September 1970 and to the Bar of England and Wales in 1974. He was a member of the Franco-British Judicial Co-operation Committee 1995-2000 and Chairman of the Distinction and Meritorious Service Awards Committee 1997-2001.

Peter McVerry is a Jesuit Priest who works with the Jesuit Centre for Faith and Justice. He has lived and worked in Dublin's Inner City and Ballymun since his ordination in 1975. He has been working with homeless young people for over twenty-five years and runs several hostels and a residential drug detox centre. He has long been critical of the State's response to homelessness and advocates the establishment of an Independent Board to respond to the problem of homeless children.

Thomas N. Mitchell was educated at University College Galway. He was awarded a PhD at Cornell University and a LittD by the University of Dublin. His early academic career was in the US at Cornell and Swarthmore, where he was appointed to a Chair in Classics in 1978. He assumed the Chair of Latin at Trinity College in 1979 and went on to hold senior administrative offices as Senior Dean and Senior Lecturer before being elected Provost in 1991. He

is a member of the Royal Irish Academy and the American
Philosophical Society and holds honorary doctorates from numerous universities.

Patricia Quinn is the Director of the Arts Council/An Chomhairle
Ealaíon, the State agency responsible for the promotion and support of the arts in the Republic of Ireland. She was previously
Cultural Director at Temple Bar Properties. Her professional life in
the contemporary arts began in the Arts Council, where for seven
years she held specialist portfolios in opera and music, and in
developing arts centres. She holds a BA (Hons) in History from
Trinity College Dublin, and a Masters Degree in Management
Practice from the Irish Management Institute/TCD. She was a member of the Forum on Broadcasting 2002.

Frances Ruane is an Associate Professor in the Department of
Economics at Trinity College Dublin. She is a graduate in economics
of University College Dublin and Oxford University. She is Chair of
the National Statistics Board, and serves on various international
advisory groups on statistics. She has also served on several Irish
State boards, including IDA, Forfás and Bord Gáis Éireann. Her
main research is on the impact of foreign direct investment on economic development and she recently co-authored *Integration and
the Regions of Europe: How the Right Policies can Prevent
Polarization*, published by the Centre for Economic Policy
Research in London.

Introduction

This book is inspired by the extraordinary career of Miriam Hederman O'Brien. What is striking is the very wide range of areas of public life in Ireland in which Miriam has made a mark; a common thread of her work has been a restless dissatisfaction with the *status quo* and a passionate desire to make things better. In Professor Joe Lee's phrase she has been on the side of the performers rather than the possessors.[1] Indeed she has regarded office not as a privilege or reward but as providing her with the opportunity and responsibility to contribute to the common good.

To celebrate Miriam's contribution to Irish life over five decades, we conceived the idea of a book of essays covering the main spheres of public life in which she has made a significant contribution. Having identified these, we invited a distinguished group of authors to contribute essays on topics related to these areas. Given Miriam's commitment to promoting change where it can improve how we manage our affairs, we asked our invited authors to make their essays forward-looking, while taking due account of current and past developments.

Many of Miriam's contributions to public life have revolved around a common theme of governance, and on how we organise our society. Where institutions have failed, it has often been due at least in part to a failure of governance. For that reason, the early chapters in this book are devoted to governance issues. The later chapters deal with particular public policy areas with which she has been concerned.

Europe

At a very early age, Miriam Hederman O'Brien was active in the European Youth campaign and she was Irish secretary of the organisation from 1954 to 1957. Over the past fifty years, she has been a passionate supporter of the project of European integration. She completed her doctorate in Trinity

College on European integration in 1980 and this led to her book *The Road to Europe,* published in 1983 by the IPA. At this time also she chaired the Irish Council for the European Movement. In 1984 she was awarded the European Order of Merit for her contribution to European understanding and integration. In the early 1990s, she held a Killeen Fellowship, which she used to study education and training interchanges between Ireland and countries in Central and Eastern Europe. In that study she stressed that '...we all need to know more about transition and the role of education and training in ensuring that it is transition for the better.' She remains an active member of the Institute of European Affairs and was editor of a study by the Institute on EU Taxation policy[2] which was published in 2002.

Given her substantial contribution to the promotion of European ideals, it seemed entirely appropriate that we ask the current President of the European Parliament, Pat Cox MEP, to consider the issue of the governance of an enlarged Europe.

Cox sets out his views on some of the most urgent and desirable reforms in European governance and also identifies some existing proposals which he believes should be ignored. Among his proposals are the following:

- that the Council of Ministers only makes law through mandated politicians and never through public servants and that laws be made in a public and transparent way
- that Ministers for Europe be appointed by the member states and share their working time between Brussels and their national legislatures. They would co-ordinate with their different national ministers and ministries in the various formations of the Council
- that in the European Parliament the specialist committees give a right of audience to national parliamentary rapporteurs for appropriate debates
- that national legislatures, borrowing from the method of the European Parliament, appoint, when they deem it appropriate to do so, a parliamentary rapporteur *ex-ante* to follow proposed EU legislative and policy initiatives

- that in the Irish context, members of the European Parliament be given a right of audience in the Houses of the Oireachtas and/or their specialist committees for appropriate debates
- that in purely Irish terms, a role be found, perhaps in Seanad Éireann, to enhance the accountability of Irish members of the European Parliament.

Cox rejects proposals for a European Senate and for the direct election of the President of the European Commission. A more workable alternative might be for the voters to choose between alternative slates of candidates for the whole Commission. However, such developments would be premature at this stage.

In relation to Economic Governance, Cox suggests that the Stability and Growth Pact needs to be revised. The limit on Government borrowing under the Pact should vary with economic cycles if this can be made to work in practice. The present Pact does not take the development needs of accession countries sufficiently into account. It requires revision to accommodate accelerated public investment programmes, subject to appropriate surveillance mechanisms at EU level. Such a change would be in the interests of all EU members, since the present rules will slow the development of the economies of the applicant countries. The only other way around this dilemma is to provide higher levels of transfers.

The Pact's 'one size fits all' approach may not be appropriate also in the case of existing Member States. Since it is concerned with long-term sustainability of public finances, account should perhaps be taken of the relative debt levels in various countries. A further factor is the widely different position of member countries regarding future pension liabilities. However, devising precise proposals about how these particular factors might be taken into account without eroding the necessary disciplines imposed by the Pact presents a particular challenge.

Cox also notes that the European Central Bank (ECB) has been granted an unprecedented level of independence. Such independence requires a similar commitment to openness, transparency and accountability. The European Parliament has consistently pushed the ECB in the direction of greater openness and transparency. Desirable steps would be the publication of summary minutes of arguments used in discussions as well as the balance of votes taken on monetary actions.

Social partnership

From 1984 to 1994 Miriam Hederman O'Brien was a prominent member of the National Economic and Social Council, as a Government nominee. This was perhaps the golden period of the Council where it laid the foundations for the development of social partnership, a partnership that has served Ireland well over the past fifteen years.

Peter Cassells, who has been a key contributor to the social partnership process in his role as Secretary-General of the Irish Congress of Trade Unions, points to its crucial contribution to the transformation of the Irish economy. Its importance was in developing a shared understanding among the social partners on the problems to be addressed, on the mechanisms for doing so, and in adopting a problem-solving approach to issues. The partners did not debate their ultimate social visions but sought to produce a consensus in which various interest groups addressed joint problems. This problem-solving approach, he argues, is a central aspect of the partnership process and is critical to its effectiveness.

For the future, he believes that the environment in which social partnership now operates is changing dramatically. The economic environment is becoming more competitive yet people are demanding better public services, the funding of which could erode our competitiveness. Industrial relations are becoming more turbulent. Increasing economic integration is accelerating the need for countries like Ireland to shift to higher skilled jobs.

As a result, the partnership agenda needs to change and expand. It must put competitiveness, increased productivity, organisational change, the adaptation of the workplace to the knowledge economy, better delivery of services and real reductions in inequality at the heart of both national and workplace policies. There also have to be stronger local and sectoral partnership and wage policies and new reward systems to reinforce this broader agenda, which creates great challenges for social partnership.

The civil service

The delivery of public services rests critically on the quality of both public servants and their organisations. An important innovation to improve the top management capability in the civil service was the introduction of the Top Level Appointments Committee in 1984. Miriam Hederman O'Brien was for many years the sole external (i.e. non public service) member of this important Committee which has overseen key changes in personnel at the upper echelons of our civil service, following the introduction of limited service terms for Secretary-Generals.

She has also conducted reviews of a number of public bodies, such as the Royal Irish Academy and the Blood Transfusion Service Board. In addition, the review of revenue administration in the fifth report of the Commission on Taxation, which she chaired, anticipated some of the key criticisms of the Revenue Commissioners identified by the Public Accounts Committee almost fifteen years later.

Paul Haran, Secretary-General of the Department of Enterprise, Trade and Employment, addresses the topic of the Civil Service in a changing world. He discusses the challenges for the Irish public sector deriving from the impact of globalisation on the Irish economy and on Irish society. Citizens are becoming more demanding and, in an increasingly globalised world, Ireland must compete more than ever to attract the international resources required to develop and retain those talented people in our society who are not content just to have good incomes. Success in the changed environment requires making Ireland an attractive place in which to live and brings quality of life issues to the fore.

Haran suggests that the public sector has a central role to play in supporting the future development of Irish society. While the forces of change are reducing the scope of public administration, they are, paradoxically, increasing the relative importance of the performance of the public service in improving national welfare. The Irish political and administrative system must constantly seek to increase Ireland's attractiveness through the range of instruments available to it. The upgrading of human capital is, perhaps, the most important challenge in this area, as both the private and public sectors are faced with greater requirements for skills that they do not currently possess. Similarly, the administrative system supporting government must also seek to improve its own performance. Haran points to the importance of having less 'silo-oriented' decision making and to the need for cross-departmental information sharing and policy development structures. He suggests that many of the management reforms now underway in the Irish public service seek to do this – only through such a process of continuous reform can Ireland hope to attract and retain the range of talented individuals required to achieve a world-class public service. He concludes by calling on the society and the political system to ensure that such ongoing reform in the public sector is both demanded and supported.

Freedom of information

In his 1953 article in *Studies*, Professor Patrick Lynch talked about the importance of public confidence in 'the quality of the official mind'. If the public believes that the management of an institution (and this applies as much in the private sector as well) is honest and competent, that institution will have much more freedom to act than one which has lost that confidence. In her various reviews of public bodies, Miriam Hederman O'Brien has promoted the need for greater transparency in how business is carried out in the public sector.

Professor Dermot Keogh charts the revolution in Irish official attitudes from rigid implementation of the Official Secrets Act to the introduction of Freedom of Information legislation in the 1990s. Together with the enactment of the Data Protection Act and the setting up of the office of Ombudsman, this revolution has helped to transform the relationship of the citizen with the State very much for the better. He suggests that the Westminster model of 'closed government' was applied in an extreme and unreformed way following Irish Independence by the early generations of politicians and civil servants. To illustrate this, Keogh recounts the attitude of the long-serving Secretary of the Department of External Affairs Joseph Walshe who, when he became Ambassador to the Holy See in 1946, reported to headquarters often under the stipulation that his reports were not to be circulated to other envoys abroad on the grounds that the contents were extremely sensitive. On a few occasions, Walshe went so far as to require that his report be shown to the Minister only and then destroyed.

Keogh notes that the Irish government was not alone in its closed culture; this attitude reflected the position of other powerful institutions such as the Church and the professions, as well as business and sporting organisations. Indeed even the media have been hostile to the idea of setting up an independent press council with the power to investigate alleged inaccuracies in media coverage.

Information is power and now that citizens have access to information held by officialdom about them, they are in a far better position to challenge the arbitrary decisions that affect them. Keogh concludes that the democratic institutions of the state were strengthened by the ultimate betrayal of the Westminster model of administration. Recent legislation to reverse this trend towards increased openness flies in the face of the move to greater democracy celebrated by Keogh.

The media

In the late 1970s, after a number of years as a commentator on international affairs on Irish radio and television, Miriam Hederman O'Brien was one of three members appointed to the Broadcasting Complaints Commission when it was established in 1977. She later became its Chairman. She has also been a member of the Advertising Standards Authority for Ireland. In these roles, she displayed a keen awareness of the important role of the media and the need for high standards.

Peter Feeney focuses on the implications for the democratic process of the changing patterns of media consumption in Ireland. Since the media are central pillars of a democratic society, with most political communication to the electorate now being through television, radio and newspapers, Irish democracy is influenced by the extent of coverage of news and current affairs in the media, and the degree to which such coverage has an Irish perspective.

Feeney notes the very significant switch of viewers from Irish to non-Irish television that has taken place over the past decade. A continuation of this trend would mean that people's exposure to debate on Irish public affairs would be limited, and in terms of world affairs, the most influential source of information would move to non-Irish television companies. The implications of this are potentially very important, he argues. As an example, he suggests that if the Irish public had acquired its understanding of the euro from British sources, the debate on Ireland joining the currency area would have been skewed by considerations largely relevant only to people in Britain.

Similar issues arise in relation to newspapers. Sales of the Irish daily broadsheets are now just over 50 per cent of total morning newspaper daily sales. Feeney argues that the market share taken up by non-Irish newspapers limits political communication and may also create an information deficit in matters essential for informed political debate.

Judicial review

The law and the Constitution provide an important check on the use of power by public bodies and officials. Miriam Hederman O'Brien is a lawyer by profession and has served as a member of the Board of the Irish Centre for European Law.

Sir Brian Kerr considers the important issue of judicial review, which is the main procedure for directly challenging the decisions of public bodies. He goes on to examine how the incorporation into domestic law of the European Convention on Human Rights and Fundamental Freedoms has altered the practice of judicial review in Northern

Ireland. This experience is of particular interest in that the Irish Government has not yet incorporated the Convention into domestic law.

He concludes that its incorporation into domestic law has enriched and extended judicial review jurisprudence. It has not, as some had feared, led to an avalanche of unmeritorious applications. Properly informed and conscientious public servants have nothing to fear from Court decisions on challenges under the Human Rights Act if they observe the fundamental and easily absorbed precepts of the Convention.

In the second part of this book the authors examine areas of public policy in which Miriam Hederman O'Brien has made a particular contribution, namely, the health services, higher education, taxation, homelessness and arts and culture.

Health services

Miriam Hederman O'Brien's contribution to health services reform and improvement has been impressive. She was chair of the Commission on Health Funding whose recommendations strongly influenced health policy in the 1990s. She chaired an enquiry into circumstances surrounding allegations of abuse against a medical consultant at Our Lady of Lourdes Hospital, Drogheda and also chaired the expert group which examined the circumstances that led to the infection of women with hepatitis C by the anti-D product produced by the Blood Transfusion Service Board. More recently, she has chaired the Joint Standing Committee of the Dublin Maternity Hospitals.

Dr Ruth Barrington deals with what she sees as serious shortcomings in the governance of the health services – at clinical level, at agency level and at health board level. She examines critically the challenges of governance at these three levels and suggests ways in which governance of the health services might be improved.

At clinical level, she points to the crucial importance of the common contract for consultants agreed in 1979. This contract effectively gives medical consultants the status of independent contractors within the health services and makes the management of medical consultants a major, and perhaps impossible, challenge. She argues that there is an urgent need for change in the consultant contract to reflect a better balance between clinical rights and responsibilities in the complex environment of a modern hospital and health system.

She points to the contamination of blood products by the Blood Transfusion Service Board with the hepatitis C virus and the delay in identifying the source of the contamination as perhaps the greatest failure of governance at agency level in the health services. To improve matters she recommends improved procedures for appointment of board members of health agencies and the introduction of regular business audits of such agencies.

As regards health boards she points to the fact that the composition of health boards in 1970 was related to the system of funding at that time, when local taxation contributed half the cost and half the members of the boards were drawn from constituent local authorities. She recommends a number of changes including direct elections to health boards from a regional constituency and the introduction of a fairer resource allocation system among health boards.

Irish universities

Miriam Hederman O'Brien's interests in higher education were reflected at many levels. She served as Chancellor of the University of Limerick 1998-2002 and has served on the Development Committee of Maynooth College for over a decade. She also led an inquiry into Letterkenny Regional Technical College. Her contributions to Irish society have been well recognised by Irish universities in the awarding to her of honorary doctorates by the NUI, the Pontifical University at Maynooth and the University of Ulster.

Professor Thomas Mitchell looks at the future of Irish Universities. He points to the substantial expansion which saw most universities more than double enrolments in a twenty-year period. He notes that the bulk of new money was directed towards new activities and strategic development in particular areas; consequently the outstanding inadequacies of central teaching and research facilities were not addressed.

Mitchell foresees a continued expansion in third-level numbers arising from the need to cater for much larger numbers of mature students; this increase will more than off-set the estimated decline in demand from school leavers. In catering for these new mature students, the state will be addressing the needs of those who originally entered the labour force at a time when fewer opportunities for third level education existed. Since a high proportion of mature students will need to continue to work (and will be needed by their employers) while pursuing their studies, courses will have to be organised in a flexible, modular form and will have to be provided outside of regular working hours. New access or bridging courses will be needed along with off-campus provision, and distance and online learning techniques, to supplement on-campus teaching.

Mitchell argues that the development of research and of a research ethos across all disciplines must be a foremost priority of all universities – it will deepen their intellectual calibre, their reputation, their capacity to attract talented students and staff, and the quality of their undergraduate and postgraduate education. For all these reasons the develop-ment of research in the universities should continue to be a priority of the state in the years ahead, building on what has been started in the 1990s.

Mitchell concludes on a sombre note – while much has been achieved in the past decade, the chronic underfunding of the Irish university system will undermine its competitive position unless addressed urgently. Without better funding there will be a slow deterioration of teaching services and intellectual endeavour. His essay suggests that the state has a major role to play in solving this problem. He also suggests that universities can address the problem of underfunding by raising private funding from the personal and corporate sectors. Finally, he proposes that underfunding can in part be addressed by 'those who can afford it' making some contribution to the high costs of an education that brings lifelong personal and professional rewards. In effect, he suggests that the issue of fees be revisited, an option recently considered by the Minister for Education and Science.

Taxation

It was her Chairmanship of the Commission on Taxation, which sat from 1980 to 1985 and produced five reports, that made Miriam Hederman O'Brien so well known to the Irish economics profession and business world. These reports were well received internationally, attracting favourable attention from such international experts as the late Professor Joseph Pechman of the Brookings Institution and John Kay, formerly Professor at the London Business School and at Oxford University, who has contributed the chapter on taxation in this volume. Her continued interest in the area of taxation and fiscal policy in general is reflected in her participation in the Foundation for Fiscal Studies, which she chaired for a number of years and in which she remains active.

John Kay argues that there are no simple principles of economic policy that are universally applicable, and hence economic institutions in general and tax policy in particular must be designed for the society of which they are part. His thesis is that 'one size does not fit all'. He considers this proposition in relation to three examples: the argument for fiscal neutrality, the relationship between taxes and benefits, and the longstanding issue of whether the chosen base for direct taxation should be income or expenditure.

Kay examines the familiar economic arguments for fiscal neutrality, pointing to their dependence on specific contextual assumptions which may not apply in practice. He reaches the conclusion that the case for fiscal neutrality rests more on the political advantages of having a coherent, defensible position against political lobbies, and of having a tax system that is administratively and legally simple to operate. The interrelationship between tax and benefits is necessarily the product of the social philosophy that underpins these structures. He draws a clear distinction between a

European benefit structure rooted in the Bismarckian concept of social insurance and the US perception of welfare as a safety net – a point perhaps relevant to the Berlin-Boston debate. In terms of the choice between income and expenditure taxation, he argues that the balance has been shifted by the changes in technology that have transformed the relative costs of comprehensive record-keeping and subjective assessment. These he sees as contributing to the evolution of the direct tax system more towards an expenditure tax rather than towards a comprehensive income tax.

It is for these reasons that the making of tax policy always demands a wide-ranging and sophisticated appreciation of the social, political and cultural context within which such policy is to be implemented. Kay concludes with the general point that policy recommendations, like the market economy itself, must always be embedded in the society of which they are part.

Homelessness

In her capacity as a member of the Board of Allied Irish Banks, Miriam Hederman O'Brien chaired the Board's Social Affairs Committee. In that role she was instrumental in establishing the AIB Better Ireland Awards which ran for ten years and were directed at encouraging community-based projects. In recent years she chaired the Forum on Youth Homelessness, whose major report published in 2000 had a very substantial impact on the proposals made in the Government's Youth Homeless Strategy published in 2001.

In a sobering chapter, Fr Peter McVerry SJ points to the doubling of homelessness in the past ten years during which Irish economic growth has been at historically high levels. Equally importantly there has been a change in its nature. He identifies two broad categories of homeless. The traditional one comprises the poor who cannot afford to provide their own homes and who are not eligible, in the short term, for public housing. The second category are those who have chronic personal problems. In the latter group are a large number of young homeless who are drug using and who are intimidating to the traditional homeless men and women who rely mainly on hostels. Many in the first category are now unwilling or afraid to accept accommodation in hostels. They fear that they may find themselves sleeping next to a drug user, or be robbed of what little they have, or be offered drugs, or be sexually molested.

A particular problem arises in relation to homeless children. Institutional problems relating to the division of responsibilities among three Government Departments and overstretched social services have contributed to the problem. McVerry points to the work of the Forum on Youth Homelessness as the way forward. The Forum recommended the creation of an Independent Board; the appointment of a Director with responsibility for homeless children; an increase in the age of young homeless who are eligible to have their needs met by the proposed new structures, from 18 to 20; the creation of locally-based multi-disciplinary teams to work with homeless young people; and the establishment of inter-linked residential placements which would promote much greater flexibility in meeting the needs of homeless young people. McVerry sees considerable merit in the strategy proposed but fears that the political commitment to implementation may not be as strong as is needed for real progress to be made.

Arts and culture

Miriam Hederman O'Brien has had a lifelong interest in music. After her Leaving Certificate, she went to Rome to pursue her music studies, before returning to study languages at UCD. In more recent years she has made significant contributions to the promotion of cultural matters as chairman of both the Irish Committee of the European Cultural Foundation and its International Executive. She is also the current Chairman of Music Network, the national music development organisation which aims to make classical, traditional and jazz music accessible to all.

Patricia Quinn reviews the development of the Arts Council since its foundation fifty years ago. From small beginnings, resources in the 1970s grew dramatically as responsibility for funding certain major cultural institutions was handed over, with their funding, to the Council.

In the 1990s significant capital funding was provided which recognised the needs of artists for permanent facilities for making, rehearsing, producing, exhibiting and performing art. The requirement for matching funding from local authorities acted as a major stimulus to the arts agenda within local government. As a result the built infrastructure for the arts locally has virtually doubled. The reform of local government has created new devolved structures that allow local priorities for arts development and support to be expressed.

For the future the Arts Council's operating environment has changed beyond recognition. There will be more focus on strategic priorities that are articulated in a measured way and policy and funding choices may not always be inclusive of all meritorious artists.

Conclusion

From this brief introduction, it is clear that Miriam Hederman O'Brien is a rare and exceptional person in the breadth of her interests and the quality of her contributions over so many fields. We are very grateful to the authors who generously responded to our invitation to contribute to this volume and we are confident that she will enjoy reading their contributions as we have done.

Notes

1 *Ireland 1912-1985 Politics and Society*, J.J. Lee, Cambridge University Press, 1989, p. 528.
2 *One Size Fits All? EU Taxation Policy*, Institute of European Affairs and Institute of Taxation in Ireland, 2002

The Governance of an Enlarged Europe

Pat Cox MEP

Introduction

The difficulties in relation to the ratification of the Nice Treaty have given us all the opportunity to reflect on the Governance of the European Union. The Institutions were designed originally for a Community of six members almost fifty years ago and have served us very well. The European project has succeeded beyond the wildest dreams of its proponents. However, many things have changed, not least the prospective enlargement of the Union, the impact of technology which makes information more accessible, increasing integration of the world economy and the social, cultural and political attitudes of citizens.

The governance arrangements for the Union have evolved over the years, most notably through the increased importance and role of the European Parliament. However, further changes are in my view necessary and in this essay, I set out my views on some of the most urgent and desirable and comment on some that I believe should be ignored.

Beware of false prophets

Before considering an appropriate governance structure, it is necessary to get one's thinking clear about the notion of national sovereignty in the European Union. Thematically the No to Nice campaign was rooted in the need to defend Irish sovereignty against the perceived ravages of European superstate federalism. Such conceptual polarities do not represent with any accuracy the effective political choices that need to be made and as such distort the debate and offer false prophecy.

Sovereignty is neither absolute nor immutable. History teaches so. In feudal Europe the monarch was absolute and sovereignty derived from God. Later in England Charles the First lost his head, God became a devolutionist and, through Parliament, sovereignty was transferred to the people, or at least to the people deemed to matter in those times. The American and French revolutions heralded the emergence of the modern state which in turn evolved through the doctrine of the separation of powers, representing a sovereignty transformed. A further adaptation was heralded with the arrival of universal suffrage less than one century ago. In short, sovereignty is not a single eternal flame but constantly has been subject to the winds of change. For our era those winds are well represented, for example by the process of European integration and globalisation and their multi-layered governance challenges.

Like truth, sovereignty is rarely pure and never simple. Exercised in its *de facto* and political form sovereignty constitutes a creative, dynamic and evolving capacity to act and to influence affairs, quite different to its more static *de jure* counterpart characteristic of a more legal mindset.

Each argument made at an extreme requires as its counterpart an extreme opposite by way of justification. In the European debate for sovereignty, the justification of absolutists derives from assertions of federalist superstate excess. For me superstate federalism is a myth. It is neither desirable nor feasible. Popular European sovereignty is member state based. Member states and in some instances their constitutional regions represent the primary source of legitimacy of the European Union. They are the repositories of civic and constitutional tradition and the expression of Europe's rich and diverse cultural heritage. Their covenant with Europe is one of sharing, not subordination. Their pooling of sovereignty has added to their capacity to act and exhibits a subtle but meaningful appreciation of the distinction between influence and control in the domain of transnational public policy. Sovereignty sharing founds itself on complementarity, not substitution. Attempting to impose a top-down superstate structure on such a complex and delicate edifice would be doomed to failure. It would propel the system towards a profound crisis of legitimacy.

False polarities and their consequential false prophecies will serve neither Ireland's public purpose nor its national interest in Europe.

Accountability and legitimacy at member state level

The Irish referendum campaigns highlighted a core question, not unique to ourselves, which will need to be addressed in future Treaty reform, i.e. how to create a greater sense of member state ownership, legitimacy and accountability of the European Union's policy process.

As a point of departure one can observe that EU legislation and policy are deeply enmeshed in the national public policy of member states. Notwithstanding this, frequently as a process it is seen as remote. In my view there are two explanations whose compound effect produces this reality. Firstly, the traditional practice in member states and in the EU has been in general to treat European Affairs as part of foreign policy. Secondly the European Union's decision-making methods typical of the Council of Ministers, which represents national interests, are closer in form to the subtleties of diplomacy than to the cut and thrust of politics. The consequence is that policy but not yet politics has been Europeanised. It is time for proposals to advance the primacy of politics over diplomacy in the European policy process.

Treating European affairs as foreign policy is significant because in all member state national parliaments such policy is a domain where the government's margin for manoeuvre and executive prerogative has been greater than for domestic affairs. National parliaments exhibit a wider and more permissive tolerance of government discretion in such matters as compared with the minute and intense scrutiny of domestic legislation. In its turn the foreign policy process relies more

heavily on the methods of diplomacy than the methods of
parliamentary politics and accountability. It is not that foreign affairs is unaccountable but rather that it is accounted
for in a significantly different way. It is no surprise that
US Presidents when hamstrung by a hostile Congress in
domestic affairs focus largely on foreign policy where they
have greater latitude.

Missing ministers

The Europeanisation of policy but not yet of politics is well
borne out by some research that the European Parliament
conducted on my behalf. For the twenty-eight months from
1 July 1999 to 12 October 2001 there were 172 meetings of
the Council of Ministers in its various formations. In more
than one case in four, specifically 27.6 per cent of cases, civil
servants and not ministers represented their states. For the
following Councils: Budget, Consumer Protection, Culture,
Development Policy, Energy, Internal Market, Telecommuni-
cations and Youth it is a story of missing Ministers, since in
more than 50 per cent of the cases civil servants alone represented their states. In four-fifths of the admittedly complex
Budget Councils no ministers attended. For the record the
best political representation is found on the Agriculture
Council where the political attendance rate is 93 per cent.

A second statistical revelation elegantly expresses the
political problem. Currently the Council has 164 working
parties and groups. In the year 2000 these bodies met on 3,537
separate occasions. Since they are defined as preparatory and
not decision-making, no official distinction is made between
legislative and non-legislative working groups, though one
may surmise that a majority of such groups are engaged in
the preparation of legislative decisions.

It is clear that in some instances the Council of Ministers in
its role as legislator devolves, one could even say abdicates,
its primary political responsibility. In a democratic order this
is not acceptable. Nor can it be accepted that when acting as
legislator the Council passes laws in private and fails to meet
the test of transparency. Occasional public sessions and

carefully honed press releases are not an adequate response to the essential democratic requirement that legislation should be made in the public view. As argued earlier the compound effect of treating European affairs as foreign affairs, added to the Council's working methods, collude to accentuate the diplomatic and marginalise the political at the heart of the European policy process. For me this begins to explain the legitimacy gap.

Some proposals for change

The reform process remains unfinished and we have an exciting opportunity to explore and articulate new preferences for the future. In the light of the above I would suggest that consideration be given to the following:

- that when it makes law the Council of Ministers only does so through mandated politicians and never through public servants
- that in making law the Council of Ministers does so on the record in a public and transparent way
- that Ministers for Europe be appointed by the member states. This should be a senior and weighty portfolio with a direct and open line of communication with their heads of government. These ministers would share their working time between Brussels and their national legislatures and in European terms would act in a law-making capacity. They would co-ordinate with their different national ministers and ministries in the various formations of the Council
- that national legislatures, borrowing from the method of the European Parliament, appoint when they deem it appropriate to do so a parliamentary rapporteur *ex-ante* to follow proposed EU legislative and policy initiatives. She/he would liaise closely with the Minister for Europe and, desirably for the relevant dossier, would assist at the relevant law-making Council in Brussels. This would enhance both parliamentary legitimacy and European policy comprehension at national level

- that in the Irish context, for appropriate debates, members of the European Parliament be given a right of audience in the Houses of the Oireachtas and/or their specialist committees
- that in the European Parliament, for appropriate debates, the specialist committees give a right of audience to national parliamentary rapporteurs
- that, in purely Irish terms, a role be found, perhaps in Seanad Éireann, to enhance the accountability of Irish Members of the European Parliament.

As an addendum to the above an additional positive consequence of appointing Ministers for Europe would be to free up the Ministers for Foreign Affairs in their role as members of the overburdened General Affairs Council, allowing them genuinely to focus on foreign policy and to move away from the process of policy co-ordination which increasingly they fail to accomplish. The creation at the Seville European Council of a new Council configuration called 'the General Affairs and External Relations Council' which staggers the meeting over successive days has not noticeably improved policy coordination. Changes are obviously still needed to underpin a transformation in member states from treating EU affairs as foreign policy to directly embedding them in national politics.

No third chamber

Many share the concern to raise the level of national political accountability of the EU policy process. Some have concluded that the answer lies in the creation of a European senate. This would be composed of members of national legislatures nominated to hold a dual mandate by their own parliament, a throwback reminiscent of the pre-directly elected European Parliament. I believe the senate proposal falls short of what is required. It risks creating the appearance of a response while side-stepping the substance of the real problem. A European senate would do nothing to make the Council of Ministers in its national context more directly accountable. The senate proposal carries the inherent risk of being and being seen to be a new political institution at the European level in search of a mission and of self definition. Moreover, it would risk overburdening an already complex EU legislative process. The European Union does not need what in effect would be a third legislative chamber. It already has a system of dual legitimacy in the respective roles, through co-decision, of the Council of Ministers and the European Parliament. In the end I believe that a European senate would add to citizens' incomprehension and confusion and in those terms would be self-defeating.

The Commission

One of the great institutional strengths of the European Union has been the role given to the Commission, which has generally over the years been a significant source of activism. Concerns about accountability have been addressed by giving greater powers to the European Parliament which, following the resignation of the Santer Commission, now can bring the Commission to account much more effectively than before.

There have been proposals that the President of the Commission might be elected directly by the people and given more powers. This proposal would I believe be completely unworkable in an enlarged Europe. For example, it is hard to imagine Irish voters being persuaded to go to the polls in large numbers to choose between say a Polish and Spanish candidate for Commission President. A more workable alternative might be for the voters to choose between alternative slates of candidates for the whole Commission. However, such developments should await a far greater degree of integration than any of us can envisage or is desirable.

A variation on the theme is the Franco-German proposal to the Convention on the future of Europe for the election of a Commission President by the European Parliament.

Economic governance

The successful launch of economic and monetary union and the introduction of the euro required new economic governance arrangements to underpin the new currency. The scale of the achievement in getting public acceptance of a new currency should not be underestimated.

The establishment of an independent European Central Bank charged solely with price stability was important in generating confidence in the new currency. Allied to this the Stability and Growth Pact, which was agreed at the Dublin summit in 1996, was designed to avoid fiscal policy undermining monetary policy. Under the Pact, eurozone member states must update their medium-term fiscal strategy every year through Stability Programmes. These are the main instruments of budgetary surveillance and are assessed by the Commission and the Ecofin Council.

Under the provisions of the Stability and Growth Pact (SGP) each Member State

> will commit itself to aim for a medium-term budgetary position **of close to balance or surplus** (original emphasis). This will allow the automatic stabilisers to work, where appropriate over the whole business cycle without breaching the 3 per cent reference value for the deficit.

The argument for a stability pact was well made by Dr Tietmayer in his address to the Institute for European Affairs in Dublin on 15 March, 1996 as follows:

> At present a country which goes heavily into debt may be penalised by the financial markets by higher interest rates. But in a monetary union all countries are affected equally, whether guilty or innocent. That is precisely why preventive agreements such as the stability pact are so important. In a single currency, a country can shift the burden of lax fiscal policy to its partners by absorbing more than its fair share of savings within the Union

and secondly by increasing the risk premium imposed by financial markets on the single currency.

He went on to argue that a stability pact is in the interest of small nations in particular. If a small country overspends, the impact on the Union as a whole and on its interest rate level is fairly small. If, on the other hand, a large country were to run extensive deficits, it would have a much more marked effect on the Union. 'A big player which errs causes much more damage than a small player.'

Two components can be identified within a current budget deficit. First, part of a deficit is explained by cycles in economic activity. During a recession, total payments to the unemployed will rise at existing rates of unemployment benefit as the numbers unemployed rise and the fall (or slower growth) in national output will reduce the buoyancy of revenue at existing tax rates. As a result, current public expenditures will rise faster than tax revenue and a current budget deficit will emerge. Second, there is that part of the current budget deficit which would still exist if unemployment was at the average level of the whole cycle in economic activity. This is the structural (as opposed to the cyclical) component of the deficit.

To a certain extent automatic stabilisers are allowed to work under the current SGP, but there may be a good case for readjusting the rules somewhat and allow for more flexibility especially for countries who respect the limits set out.

According to a communication from the Commission on 14 May 2002 some work has begun on the area of budgetary surveillance: 'significant progress has been made by the Commission and the Council towards developing an agreed method to calculate cyclically-adjusted budget balances.' Provided a satisfactory method can be agreed the use of cyclically adjusted budget deficits would be an important step forward.

The Commission followed up with a communication adopted on 25 November 2002 aimed at making the SGP more credible. It was intended to require countries with high debt levels to set down ambitious long-term reduction strategies, while creating more room for manoeuvre with regard to structural spending for countries that already respect the deficit and debt criteria of the pact.

Countries at a lower stage of development

Much more important in the context of enlargement is the need to take account of the needs of countries at lower stages of economic development. The current Stability and Growth Pact places severe constraints on borrowing for capital purposes unless the interest cost can be offset by a current budget surplus. The question arises as to whether this is appropriate for countries that require substantial investment in infrastructure to catch up with more developed countries in the Union.

The normal development model suggests that it is appropriate for developing countries to import capital. Under the Pact, such importation of capital is limited to the private sector in so far as public borrowing would have to be matched by current surpluses. The only other alternative sources of financing infrastructural investment is through transfers from the EU or public-private partnerships.

The current Stability Pact is suitable only for countries with a relatively well-developed infrastructure. It does not meet the needs of countries that require accelerated development to catch up unless we envisage massive transfers to these countries. If applied to Ireland in say, 1950, the Stability Pact would have constrained Ireland's development to an inordinate degree. The Pact clearly needs to be revised to accommodate accelerated public investment programmes in accession countries subject to appropriate surveillance mechanisms at EU level, in order to ensure that the funds are invested in projects that add to the productive capacities of the economies. Such a change would be in the interests of all EU members, since the current rules will slow the development of the economies of the applicant countries. The only other way round this dilemma is to provide higher levels of transfers.

However, it is not clear why some countries in a monetary union should be constrained to have much lower debt ratios than others. In principle, therefore, some account should be taken of growth rates in setting an annual borrowing limit, particularly as the original Maastricht criteria enable countries with slow growth rates to sustain long-run debt ratios that appear much too high.

The Pact's 'one size fits all' approach may not be appropriate in the case of existing member states. Since it is concerned with long-term sustainability of public finances, account should perhaps be taken of relative debt levels in various countries. A further factor is the widely different position of various countries regarding future pension liabilities. However, devising precise proposals about how these particular factors might be taken into account without eroding the necessary disciplines imposed by the Pact presents a particular challenge.

European Central Bank

The European Central Bank (ECB) has been granted an unprecedented level of independence. It is guaranteed legal, institutional and financial independence. The duration of the single term of office of its senior officers and their conditions are also guaranteed. It is prohibited by law from offering credit facilities to national or Community authorities. It cannot seek or take instructions from national governments. Its independence is ensured by Treaty law, ratified by all member states, and capable of change only by the ratification by all member states. Such independence requires similar commitment to openness, transparency and accountability.

The Treaty conferred on the European Parliament the task of ensuring the democratic accountability of the ECB. Three provisions determine the relationship:

- Article 109 b (3) requires the presentation of the annual report of the ECB to the European Parliament, which may hold a general debate on that basis.
- The Article also suggests that the President of the ECB and other members of the Executive Board may, at the request of the European Parliament, or on their

   own initiative, be heard by the competent committees
   of Parliament.
 • The Article also provides that the European Parliament
   must be consulted prior to the appointment by the
   Council of the President, Vice-President and members
   of the ECB Executive Board.

A good working relationship has now been established
between the ECB and the economic and monetary affairs
committee of the European Parliament. During 2002 a representative from the ECB appeared before the committee eight
times. In addition there was a hearing of candidate Papademos
and a debate in the plenary session of the Parliament when
the ECB President presented its annual report.

   The European Parliament has consistently pushed the ECB
in the direction of more openness and transparency, as it is
important for markets as well as for European parliamentarians
responsible for monitoring the bank, to understand how it
reasons when it reaches its decisions. There has been steady
progress in this field. The ECB now publishes forecasts and
has made available information about its econometric
models. Further desirable steps would be the publication of
summary minutes of arguments used in discussions as well
as the balance of votes taken on monetary action.

The Future of Social Partnership

Peter Cassells

The period since the introduction of social partnership in Ireland in 1987 has been one of unprecedented economic and social progress. Never before have we had so many people living in this country, so many people in gainful employment and so many people enjoying a standard of living that is among the highest in the world.

This contrasts strongly with the dire economic conditions that confronted the government and the social partners in 1987 when the first national programme was agreed.

Real GDP has grown on average by 9 per cent between 1993 and 2000. Employment has grown by 605,000, compared with a reduction of 76,000 from 1981 to 1987. Unemployment has fallen from 17 per cent in 1987 to 3.9 per cent in 2001. Order has been restored to the public finances with the level of public debt to GNP declining from 130 per cent in 1987 to less than 40 per cent in 2001. Also, we have been able to make long-term provisions for demographic trends (an ageing population) by providing for a national pension fund, which absorbs 1 per cent of GNP per annum.

Living standards have risen significantly, with cumulative real take-home pay for a person on average manufacturing earnings rising by over 35 per cent between 1987 and 1999. Absolute poverty has been halved and overall income levels have moved from being 60 per cent of the European average to being 118 per cent.

Reasons for this success

This successful transformation of the Irish economy can be attributed to a number of key factors, including the following:

- We have a young, growing and well-educated work-force. The quality and potential productivity of the labour force is a function of the value widely attached to education within Irish society and the level of invest-ment in education, including technological education in the 1960s and 1970s. This investment has resulted, for example, in some 80 per cent of students who enter second-level completing their leaving certificate compared with only 20 per cent who did so in 1965. Participation rates at third-level (by 18-19 year olds) have risen from 11 per cent in 1965 to over 50 per cent by the 1990s.
- There has been an increase in Foreign Direct Investment (FDI). The foreign-owned sector has made an enormous contribution to output growth, export growth and diversification, employment growth (both direct and indirect), the level of productivity and the transformation of the technological, managerial and skills base of the Irish economy. Today the foreign-owned sector accounts for over 85 per cent of manu-facturing output, some 90 per cent of exports and over 50 per cent of employment in the manufacturing sector.
- Irish companies have improved their performance in both manufacturing and services. Employment in Irish-owned manufacturing enterprises increased by more than 20 per cent between 1990 and 1998. This is not only greater than has been achieved in Ireland in the past, but in a period when there was no net growth of overall employment in the UK or the rest of the EU, it was twice the rate of employment growth in the US. The value of exports of Irish firms increased by 50 per cent between 1990 and 1998, despite slower growth in overseas markets than in the Irish economy.
- We have had a relatively benign external environment, including Ireland's membership of the European

Union. The increased integration of the Irish economy into a single European market of over 360 million people has been a major factor in Ireland's success in attracting foreign direct investment and in upgrading the performance of Irish-owned enterprise. Net EU financial transfers to Ireland, which peaked at 6.6 per cent of GDP in 1991, have helped to fund agriculture and the food sector and to upgrade investment in human and physical infrastructure. Also, the Maastricht Criteria for EMU membership and the more recent Stability and Growth Pact have imposed an important external impetus to achieving a more disciplined approach to the management of public finances on a sustained basis over time.

Contribution of social partnership

While the above factors were extremely important, most people now accept that the underpinning contribution of social partnership was a crucial element in Ireland's transition from a high-inflation, volatile and conflictual economy to a low inflation, stable economy.

It did this most obviously by providing greater certainty and stability in the whole area of pay determination, the evolution of incomes and the conduct of industrial relations. This helped to deliver moderate pay increases which improved competitiveness, enhanced the profitability of business and allowed strong economic growth to be converted into more jobs. It also delivered an improved industrial relations climate with fewer working days lost due to strikes, by educating people into realising that, while it is not possible to do away with conflicts of interest, there is a better way to do business than the old adversarial model.

It would be a mistake, however, to view the partnership process so narrowly as referring only to the negotiation of centralised wage agreements. The process also stimulated agreement on difficult economic and social priorities, brought a more coherent and consistent approach to economic and social policy, taking account of the conflicting demands on the fruits of growth, and supported in a limited way structural reform and the modernisation of the labour market.

In particular, the first Partnership Programme (1987) facilitated the formulation and implementation of government policies to tackle the public finance crisis and helped the country escape from the deep economic, social and political crisis of the 1980s. The second (1990) and third (1993) programmes prioritised employment creation over an improvement in living standards for those at work.

Subsequent programmes enabled successive governments, employers, unions, farmers and voluntary and community organisations to:

- develop a *shared understanding* on the new problems to be addressed at that time and the key mechanisms for addressing those problems; indeed, in my experience the understanding and preferences of the different players were shaped and reshaped as they interacted in this process of deliberation on key issues
- adopt a *problem-solving* approach to issues. This worked because the partners did not debate their ultimate social visions but sought to produce a consensus in which the various interest groups addressed joint problems. This problem-solving approach is a central aspect of the partnership process and is critical to its effectiveness.

The process of developing a shared understanding on key economic and social priorities and adopting a problem-solving approach to these priorities, required a recognition by the partners of their *inter-dependence*. In other words, the partnership arrangement was necessary because no party could achieve its goals without a significant degree of support from others. The willingness of government to share some of its authority with the social partners was, of course, crucial in this context. While this raised concerns about the relationship between partnership and representative democracy, over time all of the political parties came to see partnership as an extension of participative democracy.

The key to understanding why this process brought about such economic success may lie in examining the kind of consensus that was produced by the problem-solving deliberation used by the social partners. It was generally a provisional consensus to proceed with practical action, as if a certain analytical perspective was correct, while holding open the possibility of a review of goals, means and underlying analysis. It involved a dimension of hard-headed bargaining and compromise but not the form of compromise which fudges the issues that need to be addressed or the type of bargaining in which each party comes with definite preferences and seeks to maximise its gains.

While the partnership process was successful in the areas of macro-economic policy and the evolution of incomes, it has been less successful in the areas of structural reform and the modernisation of critical areas of Irish life. In particular, while some progress has been made on the Strategic Management Initiative in the public service, less progress has been made on the reform of public service pay, improving the delivery of public services and opening up of public utilities to competition. The changes needed in critical areas such as housing, health care, public transport and childcare were not anticipated and tackled and while partnership improved living standards for everyone, it also accommodated a widening disparity in incomes. Furthermore, the social partners have been less effective in developing enterprise-level partnership and modernising Irish workplaces for the future.

New circumstances

The environment within which social partnership now operates is changing dramatically. Ireland's prosperity and our achievements of recent years are at a crossroads and in a critical period of transition – with slower growth, many companies facing serious competitive pressures, growing concerns about the public finances and little scope for tax cuts to be used as an alternative to pay increases.

At the same time, people are not only demanding more resources for key services but also a much better delivery of those services. Our public services and public utilities, in particular the health services and public transport, are faced with the most significant programmes of modernisation in their history.

The general industrial relations climate is more turbulent and uncertain than at anytime for more than a decade and serious questions are being asked about the continuing relevance of partnership, in particular its capacity to generate solutions to the challenges that now face us in the new economic environment.

Indeed, as we move towards a knowledge-based economy and society, the scale of these challenges may be of a dimension different from virtually anything seen previously. The increasing integration of the economies of the world, the emergence of global companies and the dramatic growth in international financial markets have accelerated the need for countries like Ireland to shift to higher skilled, high value-added, high income jobs with a sustained increase in productivity and research and development (R&D).

Information and communication technologies have made possible the development of new systems of production and service delivery based on knowledge and information processing, and are giving us a virtual explosion in this country of new knowledge, new products, new ways of organising work and new ways of meeting human needs.

In addition, lifestyles and values are changing in Ireland, with people leading more complex lives, placing more emphasis on personal development, seeking a better balance between family and workplace responsibilities and demanding greater choice, higher standards and more flexibility in the delivery of services.

However, many aspects of government, service delivery, work organisation, industrial relations and social policy lag far behind these changes in people's values, attitudes and perceived needs.

A key question for government and the social partners is whether – especially in the new set of economic circumstances – they have the capacity to creatively cause and manage these changes and assist this country to complete the transition to a high skill, high income, fairer society with a better quality of life.

To complete this transition a number of complex tasks will have to be achieved:

- Ireland will have to become a learning, knowledge-based society with the capacity to embrace with confidence the challenges and opportunities offered by increased prosperity, the information society (including e-commerce and e-government), globalisation and social change.
- Embracing the challenge of continuing change will require all organisations and systems (including companies, unions, educational institutions, voluntary associations and systems of public policy and delivery) to be more flexible, adaptable and innovative.
- Ireland will have to accelerate the shift to high income, higher skilled, high value-added jobs with a sustained increase in productivity and R&D.
- Constraints on economic output, efficiency and social development such as the availability of infrastructure, skills and access to regulated services must be removed.
- Access must be dramatically improved to health services, public transport, childcare and lifelong learning – the quality and delivery of those services must also be radically improved.
- A procedure for the long-term reversal of inequality must be initiated.
- The coherence of the national strategy for economic and social development must be maintained in new circumstances.

Achieving this, however, will require much more than a management of our economy, including pay developments, at the national level by the government and the social partners. The agenda needs to change and the government, employers, unions and the community pillar need to develop a new and more ambitious vision that puts competitiveness, increased productivity, organisational change, the adaptation of the workplace to the knowledge economy, a better delivery of services and real reductions in inequality at the heart of national and workplace policies.

Our partnership arrangements also need to be remodelled and repositioned to develop a much stronger local and sectoral dimension to partnership linked to organisational improvements.

Implications for new direction

This new direction for partnership would have major implications for the private sector, the public service and Ireland's wage bargaining structure.

To safeguard competitiveness, increase productivity and modernise our workplaces for the future, as part of a remodelled and repositioned social partnership, managers, employees and unions in the private sector will need to co-operate to bring about:

- new and more flexible forms of work organisation that improve productivity and organisational effectiveness
- more modern workplaces adapted to the individual needs of employees, that provide lifelong learning and develop new forms of team working and project management which engage people's intelligence, commitment and energy
- a reorganisation of working time to reduce stress and to allow more time for family involvement, leisure activities and a better balance between work and life
- new reward systems (such as gainsharing, profit sharing and employee shareholding) which measure and reward good performance and recognise that, in the modern company, the knowledge and ideas of employees are as valuable as the capital of shareholders.

Developing this on-going culture of co-operation with change requires a high trust environment with employers, unions and workers acting as partners in the enterprise. This should form a key part of the next stage in the evolution of partnership in this country.

A strong local and sectoral partnership linked to organisational capability and change must also recognise that improving the delivery of public services to respond quickly, effectively and efficiently to the changing needs of the general public is now a key national priority.

There is a growing demand from the public for more and better services, particularly in the areas of health and public transport.

However, as with all services, nowadays, delivery of public services must be based on the fact that people as users are changing. They are demanding better quality, a more customised service, more information, a better response to complaints and more of a say as users in how the service operates.

Equally, public servants, as providers of the service, are changing and want more of a say in their job, more opportunities for learning and career development, greater equality and better work-life balance.

This changing environment presents enormous opportunities and challenges for public service management and unions, both externally and internally.

Externally, there is the opportunity to become one of the best public service providers in Europe of integrated solutions to problems based on customer needs (failure to achieve this, will, no doubt, lead to demands from the general public for more market-based solutions and for others to deliver these services).

The challenge, of course, is how to balance the strong centralist compliant culture of the Irish public service with a stronger 'customer/patient/pupil first' ethos and a greater understanding of good management and business practices.

Internally, in the new environment, there is an opportunity for the public service to become an employer of first choice in the country. To achieve this, public service organisations need to become learning organisations and develop a work environment that will attract, develop and retain dynamic people to work for them. New ways to reward good individual and team performance are also needed along with more effective means to deal with underperformance.

The challenge again, of course, is how to balance the centralist compliant culture with an employee development, people management ethos along with a greater devolution of authority, particularly in the area of human resource management, including pay and recruitment.

In the case of the public sector unions, there is a need to widen their focus from pay relativities and industrial relations to HR development and a better understanding of the organisation of the future. In that context, public service industrial relations procedures should be modernised and rebalanced between the central and the local to reflect the speed of change, a move to problem solving, a need to avoid disruption of service and a deepening of partnership at departmental and sectoral level.

A new direction for partnership would also have significant implications for the structure of wage bargaining.

Over the past fifteen years, Ireland's partnership arrangements have been underpinned by a fully centralised pay agreement. However, a range of factors is putting pressure on this centralised system. In recent years, higher than anticipated inflation increased wage pressures at national level, while a tight labour market exerted pressure on companies to go beyond the terms of the national pay agreement in order to meet labour shortages.

Thus, it is important to ask how a centralised wage bargaining structure can deliver appropriate wage developments at national level, while also being consistent with company-level competitiveness and an improved delivery of public services, particularly where change and adaptation at local and sectoral level may be related to pay.

The wage bargaining structure must also be responsive to developments in the international economy. In the context of EMU, the burden of adjustment to economic change is likely to fall more heavily on wage policy than ever before, given that devaluation is no longer an option. Can a highly centralised wage bargain provide the flexibility to meet a rapid short-term downturn in the economy? How will the pattern of wage bargaining in the euro zone affect monetary policy and how will Irish wage bargaining be affected by this?

Because of Ireland's experience of partnership to date, the assumption is often made that the only choice is either a fully centralised pay agreement or no partnership programme. However, there are other options and new pay architecture might be found in pay bargaining models in other European countries.

Ireland is not the only country with successful social partnership structures at present. Both the Netherlands and Denmark, for example, by adapting their structures for negotiated consensus to changing circumstances, have social partnership approaches that have achieved long-term viability.

Some countries have tried two-tier bargaining, combining agreement at central and local levels, with the second tier of pay adjustment at the local level tied to real gains in productivity, profitability and organisational performance. Alternatively, others, while retaining social partnership, attempt no more than a loose centralised co-ordination of pay adjustment in companies and organisations by agreeing centrally the criteria governing such pay adjustments.

To be successful, these forms of co-ordinated decentralisation of pay bargaining need to be coupled to reward and incentive systems built around enterprise partnership, with a shared understanding between employers, employees and unions that co-operative working relationships are the key to higher organisational and business performance.

Conclusion

There can be no doubt about the enormous contribution that the series of social partnership programmes over the last fifteen years has made to the dramatic transformation of the Irish economy and indeed society. The importance of these programmes has transcended the terms written in agreements, they have represented an inclusive, problem-solving approach to addressing difficulties facing society as a whole and they have enriched the public policy-making process.

Partnership, however, only has a future if it continues to be consistent with the dynamic of the economy and of Irish society and if it can actively create change and help to solve the problems which change throws up.

The problems Ireland now faces are in certain ways more difficult to address than those of the past. Back in the late 1980s, the solutions were simple in the sense that there was a clear macro-economic/fiscal route to be followed based on pay moderation and tax reductions in a low inflation environment, linked at a later stage to social inclusion measures based on particular areas of public expenditure.

The current problems are more complex. They cannot be tackled at the national macro-level as part of an overall rigid centralised agreement nor, as health care has shown, will additional resources in themselves lead to solutions.

The challenge facing government and the social partners is to continue to experiment with the partnership process and in that context to:

- remodel the partnership agenda to tackle the key priorities of organisational change, competitiveness, increased productivity, a better delivery of public services and real reductions in inequality
- reposition partnership around a stronger local and sectoral partnership to achieve higher organisational performance and develop the workplace of the future
- underpin this new direction for partnership with a suitable wage policy and new reward systems that reinforce this agenda.

Success in achieving these tasks will have a major influence on the depth and durability of this country's new-found prosperity and on Ireland's attempts to create an enterprise society with social solidarity.

References

NESC (1990), *A Strategy for the Nineties: Economic Stability and Structural Change*, Dublin: National Economic and Social Council

NESC (1996), *Strategy into the 21st Century,* Dublin: National Economic and Social Council

O'Donnell R. (2001), *The Future of Irish Social Partnership,* Dublin: National Competitiveness Council

O'Donnell R. and O'Reardon C. (1997), *Ireland's Experiment in Social Partnership 1987–96 in Social Pacts in Europe,* Brussels: European Trade Union Institute

O'Donnell R. and Thomas D. (1998), *Partnership and Policy-Making in Social Policy in Ireland,* Dublin: Oak Tree Press

O'Donnell R. (2000), 'Public Policy and Social Partnership' in *Questioning Ireland,* Dublin Institute of Public Administration

Roche W. (2002), 'Time to build workplace partnerships whatever about national partnership', *Irish Times,* 25 April

NCPP (2002), *Modernising Our Workplaces for the Future – A Strategy for Change and Innovation,* Dublin: National Centre for Partnership and Performance

3

The Irish Civil Service in a Changing World

Paul Haran

Introduction

Ireland's future welfare depends on how it responds to a changing environment.

There are several forces driving change:

- the growing level, and penetration, of globalisation
- the increasing liquidity of many key factors of social and economic life
- the quickening pace of technological advance
- a citizenry that is demanding an enhanced level of services.

The nature and impact of these different forces are reviewed below and an assessment is made of the challenges which they will pose for Ireland's social and economic development, for government and in particular for the management of the Irish public service.

This chapter suggests that while the forces of globalisation may be reducing the reach of national administrations, the performance of these administrations is becoming increasingly important in determining future national welfare. The chapter goes on to sketch a change agenda.

Globalisation

Globalisation is perhaps the most powerful and pervasive driver of change impacting on national governments today.

It affects many aspects of the life of a country and its people including cultural identity, social development and economic well being. Globalisation changes the scope and relevance of national physical and political boundaries. Ireland, in common with most countries, has traditionally operated with considerable sovereignty over most economic, communications, and trade levers. However, these traditional arrangements are changing rapidly under the impetus of a number of forces.

Pooling of sovereignty

In common with many nations, Ireland pools its sovereignty through various international agreements. These include the treaties and related instruments of the European Union, the Good Friday Agreement, membership of a wide range of international protocols and institutions such as the International Labour Organisation (ILO), the United Nations (UN), the Council of Europe and the World Trade Organisation (WTO). This deepening interdependence has significantly reduced the number of areas where Ireland can act independently and has changed radically the decision-making environment. The pooling of sovereignty has also deepened and broadened Ireland's role in international affairs.

Impact of technology

Complementing this political change has been a communications revolution that has considerably reduced the relevance of geography. The dramatic developments in information and communications technologies, driven by Moore's Law, have transformed activity in many areas: from trading derivatives across global capital markets to viewing world entertainment events live. Significant changes in the structure of air transport have also led to a dramatic increase in global travel.

New industrial structures

In the industrial area, truly global companies are emerging where both the workforce and management are multi-ethnic.

Culture is more likely to be corporate than national. Operations including sales, production, distribution and the research and development functions are to be found in disparate locations. Frequently the ownership base is also global, through the holdings of individuals and their international investment and pension funds. Managing the relationship with these global companies is a challenge for national administrations.

Global markets

International trade has expanded enormously in recent years, with total world merchandise exports increasing by over four thousand billion dollars in the 20 years to the year 2000, more than tripling in value. It is estimated that the value of foreign direct investment in 2000 was about one and a half thousand billion dollars. The daily trade in inter-national financial markets is measured in trillions of dollars per day. Just as the domestic marketplace requires regulation, global markets need regulatory structures and institutions to ensure their efficient operation. Investors and consumers alike need to be assured that anti-competitive practices are thwarted, that intellectual property is protected, that fair market access is provided and that exploitative behaviour is discouraged. Market-based mechanisms alone cannot adequately provide the appropriate level of protection. New international regulatory structures that have robust political and administrative connections to citizens and governments are required and are emerging.

Non-governmental organisations

Similarly a growing number of global non-governmental bodies is also emerging. While some are specifically anti-globalisation in intent, most seek to deal with consumer, labour, trade and environmental issues on a global basis. These bodies are managed and operate in a way that again does not mirror traditional political and geographic bound-aries. The growing importance and influence of such bodies present particular challenges for national and international political and administrative institutions to work with.

Liquidity

The dramatic increase in the liquidity of many important factors of economic and social life is driving change. The term liquidity is used here to describe the capacity of important factors to diffuse globally or be exploited rapidly across the world with a minimum of friction or impedance. Coupled with the forces of globalisation and technological development this amounts to a revolution of change.

Knowledge and ideas know no boundaries

Technological innovation and knowledge have become the key value-adding aspects of production and wealth creation. Knowledge can cross the globe with few constraints, especially aided by the new communications facilities.

People less tied to locations

The movement of people around the globe has become easier and cheaper. It has also become easier to use workforces remotely from central activity. Large companies, using new communications technologies, may use cheaper labour or a plentiful supply of particular skills where they exist rather than bring workers to the central facilities. They can bring the work to people rather than people to the work on a global basis. Both Ireland and India have exploited this opportunity well. The emergence and development of tele-working is also pioneering new work models that may be less constrained by traditional physical boundaries. These factors, coupled with the increased liquidity and importance of knowledge, will result in human-capital itself becoming considerably more liquid.

The example of capital markets

The transformation of capital markets in recent years is an interesting example. Physical and political boundaries have become virtually redundant in the face of global flows of capital. Modern communications and financial product innovation have revolutionised the liquidity of these markets.

National governments have learned that they cannot staunch the capital flows out of countries or currencies. Markets can and do respond immediately to shocks wherever they occur. Vast resources flow at electronic speed and highly sophisticated systems have been developed to manage any risks and optimise returns. This has led to the achievement of significant economic efficiencies by enabling resources to flow quickly to projects offering higher returns wherever they exist. These markets and the increased liquidity of capital create new and at times enormous pressures on national and international political and administrative systems.

Culture under threat?

There is a fear that globalisation will undermine national cultural identity. Ideas, fashion, music and other forms of cultural expression are also subject to this increased liquidity, and global media companies have emerged. These trends raise the concern that national and regional cultural identities might be subsumed by a globalisation or homogenisation of culture, that a *Hollywood* type global dominance in the entertainment industry could be at the expense of richer cultural diversity. Against this, others argue that these technologies are also facilitating the emergence of virtual systems to support and propagate culture such as the availability of ethnic TV, Internet and film channels across the world to national or ethnic diaspora. It is also argued that culture is enriched by the enhanced liquidity and competition of ideas, music and other art forms.

A changing Ireland

Under the influence of these powerful external drivers of change Irish society will be forced to adjust irrespective of any conscious actions by its political and administrative system. However, Ireland can make choices to harness these global forces for the betterment of its people and ensure that it competes well to be the best place in which to live and work.

More demanding citizenry

The attitude of Irish people is also changing significantly and this is set to continue. The population is expanding, its age profile is changing and it is becoming more ethnically diverse. People are now more likely to recognise and assert their rights than ever before. International media and travel have exposed people to new ideas, service excellence, and best-practice models that they increasingly demand at home. Increased levels of education and new citizen support structures have empowered people in affirming and securing their rights. Higher levels of material and financial affluence have broadened and made more complex the set of responses that individuals demand from the state. New representational and advocacy structures have also given certain groups of citizens enhanced power and leverage in dealing with the state.

Emphasis on attracting

As the parallel forces of globalisation and liquidity blur national political, economic and geographic boundaries an enormous and continuing effort will be required to *attract* that which was once assumed as *captured*. This applies particularly in a small, exceptionally open and rapidly growing economy such as Ireland.

For example, indigenous companies that in the past, because of ownership, financial and consumer structures, may have been considered immobile are now, and will increasingly become, internationally mobile. The key determinant of choosing a location for individual citizens to live in, as well as for businesses to operate from, will be the *relative* attraction of one particular location against another. Countries and regions increasingly have to compete to make themselves the most attractive location for knowledge workers, for artists, for capital and financial investment, for production and for service provision.

Making Ireland a better place in which to live

Making Ireland a better place to live in is a core challenge. It is central to Ireland's future economic welfare but also to the continued well-being of its people. This has always been a desirable goal in itself and a focus of government policy. What has changed is firstly, the more explicit nature of the challenge, secondly, the increased importance of the concept of *relative* attractiveness and thirdly, the fact that the cost of failure is becoming more acute and obvious with the increased ease of movement of activity *out* of locations.

People are the key

Ensuring that the country is attractive to companies through such areas as competitive fiscal systems, high quality infrastructure and efficient regulatory structures, is necessary but not sufficient. Despite the increased mobility of people, the quality of a location's workforce in the context of the knowledge economy is, increasingly, the most important determinant in securing mobile investment and high-value activity. The continued upgrading of the workforce through significantly enhancing our education systems, through securing a practice of lifelong learning and through transforming our research and innovation performance is fundamental.

Quality of life important

It will be essential for the country to continue to be the location of choice for its own citizens especially those who are more mobile than others. High achieving students, high performing researchers and sought-after artists all face attractive alternatives across the globe. Therefore Ireland must ensure that it delivers well on quality-of-life factors and remains an attractive location so as to retain its own mobile workforce and encourage others who are best in their field to locate in Ireland.

The challenge agenda

Many of the features that determine the attractiveness of Ireland to its citizens, and those who might join it, are influenced by the administrative actions of its government and public service. These range from the basic set of public services such as security and welfare, to a broad span of quality-of-life factors such as culture and recreation.

Ireland's administration faces a number of challenges in the context of these forces. It will be important to remain nimble and agile in the face of continuous and unexpected change so that opportunities can be seized and threats responded to. Ireland will also have to demonstrate a new capacity to deliver both large-scale infrastructural projects and significant policy changes that have medium to longer term delivery horizons. This will require leadership to identify, articulate, and secure a shared vision for the future and then harness the resources to secure its delivery across a wider planning and budgeting environment.

It will also be necessary to determine the appropriate role of national government in an arena of:

- different and perhaps competing tiers of government, both local and international
- alternative systems of delivery between the public and private sectors.

This will be a significant challenge.

Remaining nimble

Ireland's agility and responsiveness represent a formidable strategic strength. Social partnership has helped ensure that there is a shared understanding of the challenge agenda. The intimacy of Irish society and its relatively informal structures enable effective and efficient communication. These factors, coupled with the evolution of the Irish political system, have supported a tradition of pragmatism in problem solving rather than a doctrinaire one, and consequentially one with less swings in policy. This policy consistency and general coherence gives considerable confidence to external investors and has yielded dividends.

Leadership

Providing the leadership to ensure that Ireland is ready for the global developments taking place is important. The challenge of seeking to influence the external environment while managing the internal response is a sensitive process. Those countries that manage it effectively stand to make considerable gains by ensuring a smoother adjustment for their societies.

Long-term project delivery

A strategic challenge facing Ireland is to ensure that the necessary infrastructure – with an appropriate price/quality profile – is in place when needed. To achieve this, new systems of anticipating, planning and delivering long-term projects across a range of infrastructure must be developed. This requirement is not limited to large-scale capital projects but would also cover such areas as the education system where a significant time lag exists from the investment/policy decision to the ultimate output stream.

Public or private provision?

Determining the correct balance between public and private sector provision is another challenge facing government. Technology and growing private sector capacity are opening-up new opportunities for private sector involvement in the delivery of services that were hitherto considered as within the exclusive domain of the public sector. The successful involvement of the private sector in the transport and communications sectors, where competitive markets can be organised, demonstrates the possible consumer gains. However, the public service can also adopt private sector practices to significantly upgrade the services it provides, and at times provide best-practice leadership. The E-Government project now underway in the Irish civil service aims to do this.

Subsidiarity

A related challenge is determining the optimum tier of government to provide or secure service provision. This is not immutable and can change as technologies and new mechanisms allow. At national level, government is being

pulled in both directions. In one direction, there is the movement of some responsibilities to higher/supranational tiers of
government such as monetary policy going to the ECB. In
the other direction, there is the demand and the opportunity
to provide lower tiers of government, such as local authorities
and indeed other groups within the community, with more
responsibility. Principles of subsidiarity and political economy
would generally favour locating service provision as close to
the citizen/consumer as possible. There is also the significant
democratic challenge of ensuring that the tiers of government,
or body, responsible for service delivery have an appropriate
connection with the citizens they serve. These challenges are
very considerable.

International influence

Ireland must continually improve the way it works with the
many supranational bodies, especially the EU, that play a
major role in its environment. Identifying, pursuing and
securing strategic, tactical and operational priorities across
the complex web of international institutions pose a considerable challenge. This will require continuous investment. As
a small country, prioritising the use of leverage and resources
will be important. However, Ireland may also economise by
'piggybacking' on the Union's position and, perhaps, on its
institutions in some areas rather than through its own direct
involvement. For example this is increasingly the case in the
area of multi-lateral trade negotiation.

The public service challenge

This agenda will demand a continuously improving public
service. The administrative system will be faced with a
growing set of complex tasks in an environment where it has
less direct control. Ireland's future welfare will depend on its
capacity to secure excellence in its civil and wider public
service. Driving the public service to best-in-the-world status
will be one of the main ways of ensuring that Ireland is the
most attractive location in which to live, grow, work and
produce.

Right-sizing the public service

Best-in-the-world does not equate with being the largest or most pervasive. It is up to the political system to determine the appropriate balance between providing services, redistributing resources, and taxation. Best-in-the-world status will demand that the Irish public service secures the best output/quality mix deliverable within whatever resource allocation is decided.

Upgrading the public service

The challenge is a dynamic one. It is to *continually* upgrade performance in the public service. The Strategic Management Initiative (SMI) has been a major driver of such change – it has provided solid foundations. The alternative title to SMI, *Delivering Better Government*, captures in a more coherent way the true challenge facing the Irish civil and public service. *Better Government* means improvements that are planned, measurable and time-bound. They must make a significant and demonstrable impact within the public service and more importantly for its citizens. Such a process must have a strong and sustained political drive, which can only happen if its importance is recognised and the public service rises to the challenge by delivering continuous improvements.

People again the issue

The challenge of growing performance rests around people and to a lesser extent structures. Attracting and retaining high quality people will be essential as will be the management of performance. The public service will need to challenge, grow, train, acknowledge and reward its own staff if it is to compete successfully against other employments. Critically, it must address underperformance more effectively than it has done to date. Failing to address the persistent and obvious underperformance of a very small number of people is a pervasive problem throughout the public service and a major impediment to a fairer workplace. This needs to be addressed in a just way that recognises the rights of the underperformer, those other members of staff who are per-forming well and often carrying the additional workload of the underperformer, and the taxpayers. The human resource function and practices need to be upgraded accordingly.

Need to break the cycle of paying for change

Public service organisations invariably have a large number of grades, often of different streams, that operate in a strongly hierarchical way. The combination of this structure and the grade-based organisation of the workforce can be too inflex-ible in a changing and challenging environment.

Too frequently what is managed as a human resources issue in modern enterprises is treated as an industrial rela-tions issue in the public service. This is usually characterised by repeated claims for payment for change and grade demar-cation issues. The number of levels and the multiplicity of rules impede the flexible deployment of people to the detriment of efficiency.

The new partnership model is helping to introduce new ways of working together and avoid the perhaps more traditional adversarial model of dealing with change. Much more needs to be done in this area to secure best practice.

New employment options

Recruitment is predominantly by entry at the lowest point of a stream. Current practice supports high-performing staff moving to the private sector, through such arrangements as career breaks, but does not allow the reverse. This can only contribute to a drain of excellence.

Permanent employment is likely to remain the career norm in the public service. It offers an environment where a public-service ethic can be encouraged and where the expertise necessary to deliver at the highest level can be nur-tured. Nevertheless an agile and responsive environment needs a public service that is itself both agile and able to respond to new challenges in a positive way.

The public service cannot wait to grow skills when they are needed immediately. Neither can it solely rely on its generalist staffing to provide the specialist skills required in an increasingly complex environment. To address this, new recruitment options across all levels and streams are needed with a greater two-way flow between the public and private sectors. The public service should be able to tap the wider economy for its top-level management. In doing this, the Irish public service needs to have the maturity and the confidence in its own capacity to compete for these positions in the open market place.

Encouraging diversity

It is also likely that the Irish public sector could be enriched and made more effective if there was more recruitment from outside traditional ethnic or national norms. It is desirable that the composition of the public sector reflects the diversity of the society it serves. It is also important that, as the public service seeks to enhance its capacity to influence supranational bodies, it can also call on a broader set of skills and understandings.

Performance management

One of the key enablers of an effective human resource practice is performance management (PM). Currently being implemented, PM seeks to align an organisation's business plans with an individual's work assignment and personal development plan. The development plan is regarded as an integral part of this process, recognising the importance of the 'people' dimension. This framework ensures that tasks are made explicit and provides a structure where performance is reviewed and new objectives agreed. PM along with the development of strategy statements and annual business plans is now bringing a greater focus on performance indicators, on output measures and, as we move forward, on outcome reviews.

Resource management

New financial resource-management structures, such as the management information framework (MIF), are being developed to support this new environment. These initiatives are placing an increased emphasis on growing management capacity and delivery performance. They seek to link in a coherent way the deployment of resources, money and people, with the delivery of specified planned outputs. These outputs would then be reviewed to ensure that the outcomes being pursued were realised. A simple example would be linking the expenditure in a policing district (in terms of the deployment of gardaí and other resources) with a level of planned police output (numbers on the beat, checkpoints, etc) and then checking the impact on the crime levels in the area (outcome). The public service will have to develop new skills to measure outputs and analyse outcomes.

Need to encourage new approaches

Performance management seeks to improve training and learning systems. Nevertheless, success and failure are often treated in an unbalanced or asymmetric way, where fear of failure can dominate. This can stifle innovation and entrepreneurship and impede improvement. Given the emphasis on the need to change and improve performance we must guard against this tendency.

The need to try out new solutions, new services or ways of providing such services, must be supported. Innovation must be encouraged and rewarded. We must identify failed approaches without concluding that those who innovated are failures. This requires a more sophisticated and mature approach to public service management and accountability.

Open and transparent structures that welcome self-critical analysis are more likely to correct failure early on, more likely to learn and share their learning and more likely to improve and innovate successfully. The corollary is that if the system has inbuilt structures that seek out and concentrate on failure, then innovation and improvement may be inhibited.

A new emphasis on quality

Growing quality must be a pervasive requirement of the change agenda. This is how locations are distinguished internationally. Quality means doing both the simple and the hard things effectively and efficiently on a consistent and professional basis. Quality deficiencies cost in the longer term and reveal a lot about an organisation's capability. We must reach out to secure higher improvements in quality customer service across the public service.

Yet, quality programmes where resources are limited require organisations to concentrate on agreed priorities and dropping other less urgent or important activities. Agreeing the resource, quality and span configuration for our public sector organisations is a major challenge. Getting it wrong will lead to a loss of confidence both within these organisations and their citizens. Failing to do so will facilitate poorer performance.

Transformation needs to involve everyone

These changes provide the building blocks for a transformation of our public service. The developments need to be rigorously pursued to enable the public service to significantly enhance its performance and focus. To deliver this will require new relationships between the public sector deliverer, government and public representatives. Everyone has a part to play in securing this dynamic. The citizens, the boards of our state companies, the councils of our local authorities, and the Oireachtas must both demand and support the transformation process, in the knowledge that our economic and social welfare depends on it.

Conclusion

The public sector has a central role to play in supporting the future development of Irish society. While the global forces of change are narrowing the ambit of government, they are paradoxically increasing the relative importance of the performance of the pubic service in improving national welfare.

The Irish political and administrative system must constantly seek to make Ireland the best place to be in through the range of instruments available to it.

Securing a culture of systemic and constant improvement in the performance of the public service is at the heart of this challenge. Many of the reforms now underway seek to do this. However, significant challenges remain and tangible improvements need to be identified and delivered urgently if the system's capacity to improve itself is to be proven.

We also need to ensure that the public service inculcates and supports innovation and entrepreneurship within. New challenges may require new and imaginative solutions. Novel approaches may have to be tried and some traditional approaches abandoned.

Society and its political system must ensure that a programme of ongoing reform and improvement is demanded, supported and delivered. Ireland's outstanding performance in recent years demonstrates its capacity to deliver on this challenge.

4

Citizenship and the Irish Freedom of Information Revolution

Dermot Keogh

Introduction

The legal basis and general climate for the study of twentieth-century Ireland has changed dramatically for the better over the past three decades. The shift has been so dramatic that it may be possible to refer to the Irish freedom of information 'revolution.' From being one of the most reactionary countries with regard to access to official state records, Ireland is now very much like most other countries of the European Union. It is not as advanced as Sweden or Holland but it resides comfortably in the upper sector of the league table of the member states.

The legal framework governing an Irish citizen's right to know has been carefully laid down in less than a decade. Access to official archives and government material now operates under a thirty-year rule. The National Archives Act, 1986 has, for reasons I will explain later, completely changed the legal basis of the world of the professional historian engaged in the study of the Irish state. That legislation has also helped shift the climate in which the investigator operates. Doors that remained closed to the files of government departments until the 1970s, in the case of the Department of the Taoiseach, and much later for other government departments, have now been unlocked. The culture of openness, let it be called, has been further strengthened by the operations of the Data Protection Act, 1988 and the Freedom of Information (FOI) Act, 1997. The setting up of the office of Ombudsman in 1980 gave teeth to that growing body of legislation which reinforced the culture of openness.

The combined effect of the operations of the Office of the Ombudsman in the context of the three pieces of legislation mentioned above has, in my view, helped to transform the relationship of the citizen to the state very much for the better. What has transpired is little less than a freedom of information revolution. As an historian and as a citizen I have cause to be grateful to the civil servants and to the politicians who helped bring this silent revolution to pass.

Opposition to the change

It would be quite correct to suggest that the struggle to create a culture of openness in Irish society was done against the wishes of a monolithic civil service wholly antagonistic to the process. There was strong resistance to the introduction of the National Archives Bill. When the idea was first mooted during the time of the Fine Gael/Labour Coalition of 1973-77, the Taoiseach Liam Cosgrave had to press very hard to make the first breach in the wall of hostility to the transfer of files to the then Public Records Office, Four Courts, and the State Papers Office, Dublin Castle. Resistance was very stiff indeed. Cosgrave simply drove it through his department and the historic transfers were made. The idea of files belonging to the Department of the Taoiseach being deposited in repositories where they could be inspected by the public became the norm in the late 1970s and 1980s. The National Archives Act was not finally placed on the statute books until 1986.

The fact that the thirty-year rule was the norm in North America and in most member states of what is now called the European Union ought not to detract from an acknowledgement of the administrative/political achievement that the passage of that piece of legislation signified in this small country. A particularly conservative mind-set pervaded the Irish civil service. Why should an historian, or a citizen for that matter, be entitled to see official documents? They were the working files of the civil service. But the answer was quite simple. The right was implicit in one's Irish citizenship – a right acknowledged by most other member states of the then European Community. What an alarming thought, particularly if one had spent a lifetime being too-clever-by-half writing memoranda and minutes which one might not ever wish to stand over in the clear light of day.

It is little wonder that Mr Cosgrave and his successors encountered such incomprehension in the civil service when the idea of an archive Act was first mooted. But there was also a reforming current in that same civil service that facilitated the passage of the revolution. The thirty-year rule is now a reality and has been so for over a decade. The civil service world has not ended to the best of my knowledge. If it has not ended, the world of closed government in Ireland is under constant pressure. The demand for change grows.

Radical legal changes, which have greatly enhanced the rights of the citizen, were made possible by both external and internal factors. Externally, the international culture of governance in North America, Australia and New Zealand has moved strongly in the direction of openness. The operation of legislation on freedom of information in those jurisdictions has strengthened the right of the citizen to know. Within the European Union, there has been a studied attempt to redress the 'democratic deficit'. Scandal and the lack of transparency in the workings of the Commission set in train a new process of institutional reform. President Romano Prodi has successfully overseen the beginnings of that reform. The European Parliament, including MEPs like Pat Cox, helped bring that reform to pass in the 1990s. Access is now easier in 2002 to official EU documentation and the records of the Commission and the Council of Ministers, together with the working papers of the committees of the European Parliament.

Significant strides have been made to break down the barriers posed by excessive bureaucracy in the EU. The role of the European Parliament, under its President, Pat Cox, is likely to accelerate that pace of reform and further enhance citizens' rights. It is inaccurate to describe the influence of the EU as an 'external' factor. With the accession of Sweden to the EU, the move towards greater transparency and openness has intensified. As a member state of the EU, Ireland now shares a common currency and, perhaps more importantly, a common citizenship with her partners. The Irish government will continue to find that there is growing pressure from the EU institutions to deepen the country's freedom of information culture.

Culture of secrecy

The Irish State, a bastion of classical bureaucratic conservatism for most of the twentieth century, could not have avoided being affected by such dramatic international changes. The Westminster model of closed government was applied in an extreme and unreformed way by the early generations of politicians and civil servants in the new state. The civil war divide made little difference to the philosophy of bureaucratic politics shared by Cumann na nGaedheal/Fine Gael and Fianna Fáil. The British model, despite earlier intellectual interest during the War of Independence between 1919 and 1921 with the US and the Swiss, prevailed. Paradoxically, that was as much the case in departments that were inherited by the new state from the British period as it was for the newly established departments like External Affairs and Defence.

The Department of External Affairs under its long-serving secretary, Joseph Walshe, was a model of closed government. The latter was effectively in charge of the department between 1922 and 1946. He had no direct experience of the British administrative system. He joined the revolutionary movement as a diplomat in 1919. He was a barrister by profession, his earlier formation having been for over ten years as a Jesuit seminarian and scholastic.

Walshe worked with Seán T. O'Kelly in Paris before being transferred back to headquarters in Dublin where he was first acting secretary and then secretary, a position he held until he became Ambassador to the Holy See in 1946. He worked closely with Desmond FitzGerald, Kevin O'Higgins, William T. Cosgrave and Patrick McGilligan – all holding the position of Minister of External Affairs between 1922 and 1932 – and developed a particularly close working relationship with Éamon de Valera who was the Minister for External Affairs between 1932 and 1948. Both men shared a common preoccupation with secrecy, which worked against the more efficient running of the department.

When he became Ambassador to the Holy See in 1946, the former secretary reported to headquarters often under the stipulation that his reports were not to be circulated to other Irish envoys abroad. The rationale was that the contents of the reports were extremely sensitive. On a few occasions, Walshe required that his report be shown to the minister only and then destroyed. The Secretary of the Department, Frederick Boland, did not carry out Walshe's instructions. The ambassador's reports, marked 'destroy', remain on the file.

If Walshe was sensitive about allowing senior ranking Irish diplomats access to certain departmental documentation, it would have been unthinkable for a man of his mind-set to conceive that files containing such state secrets would ever be made available to the public under a thirty-year rule. He died in the mid-1950s and did not live to see the introduction of the thirty-year rule. But his spirit lived on in some sections of the department until the 1980s. I will relate my experience in that regard later.

Historically, the administrative practices of the Irish State reflected and reinforced the closed culture of other powerful institutions in the country. Other bodies, such as the Catholic Church and other churches, shared a similar mind-set to the early generations of ministers and senior civil servants. The professions, in particular the medical profession, were both self-regulating and practitioners of closed government. Other major Irish institutions such as the national army, banking and business and even sporting organisations were equally closed in their administrative practices. Even the journalistic profession in Ireland – so loud a protagonist for the intro-duction of FOI legislation – has paradoxically been hostile to the idea of setting up an independent press council with the power to investigate alleged inaccuracies in media coverage.

With certain rare and limited exceptions – and journalism was an exception – all those named institutions enjoyed the certitude of being able to work on a day-to-day basis in a

world hermetically sealed from the general accountability that
follows upon the opening up of relevant documentation. In
the end, who was responsible? Why, the institution of
course. Citizens, inquiring about issues of major personal
importance, usually hit a brick wall of officialdom. Those
who took decisions at variance with the rights of a citizen
could take refuge in the anonymous world of the institution,
be it a government department, a commercial institution or
a church. There was always a veil to hide behind.

An official would refuse to give a full name on the telephone. The signature at the end of a letter from a government department was sometimes indecipherable. Letters
might often go unacknowledged and unanswered. A citizen
might be told that a letter had never been received. If it had
been hand-delivered or sent by registered post, then the file
might have temporarily 'gone missing'. A file might be
'grand-fathered' – such a phrase I heard not so long ago
being used by a civil servant. I think that had the meaning
of being buried under an amorphous pile of files where it
would languish until the present danger had passed.
Alternatively, the citizen might be offered the lame excuse
that the correspondence had been put on the wrong file and
a search was in progress. But did the search produce speedy
results? Not usually. The citizen was left in the dark.

But the gravity and injustice of the situation is only fully
realised when one considers that a citizen was likely to be
treated not only by government but by other institutions in
the state in the self same manner. Local authorities often
replicated the worst practices of central government. The
arrogance that pervaded national and local administrative
structures was also to be found in the church, in banking and
commercial institutions and in the professions. Under FOI,
the legal acknowledgement of the right of an Irish citizen to
gain access to official documentation relating to himself/her-
self has challenged and is changing such practices. The right
to such information always existed in natural justice. But the
Irish State did not acknowledge, usually for reasons of
national security, that it was obliged to make the relevant
files available to the citizen.

That attitude pervaded the working of the civil service and local government for most of the century. I have often wondered how many candidates were not permitted to take up positions in the public service because they had not passed a 'security' clearance. The legitimacy of such concerns is not in dispute. But there is a significant difference between somebody who has become a member of an oath-bound subversive organisation and a student/worker who might have had a mild and short-lived flirtation with revolutionary politics. What right did the latter have over the decades to correct the contents of his/her personal file? The answer was that the person did not get the opportunity because of reasons of state. Such blunt considerations may have resulted in the blighting of many promising administrative careers.

In the absence of detailed research, it has yet to be ascertained how many people in Ireland during many decades of the twentieth century have been the victims of arbitrary decisions at the hands of institutions other than the state. How many seminarians were obliged to leave a religious order without an explanation or were denied ordination without a reason? How many bank officials were transferred or were dismissed without adequate explanation? What place did snobbery and class play in both admission to the banks and determining promotion?

There are many similar questions that might be asked of other institutions in the state. But those latter institutions – particularly the Catholic Church – appear to have lost their imperial status during the 1980s and 1990s. A disturbingly large number of male and female religious in the Catholic Church were confronted by allegations of child sexual abuse. There were good grounds for asking questions about the manner in which religious orders conducted the running of state-funded industrial schools and orphanages in their care. The range of such charges stretched back over decades. The national TV station, RTÉ, broadcast two series on the subject of the Catholic Church and child neglect, sexual abuse and the use of violence. There were a number of court cases involving charges of pederasty against members of the diocesan clergy and male and female religious. The question was repeatedly asked: 'How could this have happened?'

The answer is complex and requires much research. Too many times over the past few years there has been a rush to judgement in these matters by media and other sources. The 'church' is a relatively easy target at a time of growing anti-clericalism. The role of the state has been too often marginalised in those circumstances. Certainly, part of the answer to the question posed was that the continuation of such practices was greatly enhanced by the worst features of closed government in the running of church affairs. However, discussion about those matters reinforced the demands for change and for greater transparency and accountability in the running of the affairs of both church and state.

Banking, a bastion in Ireland of probity and high standards, was also under scrutiny in the 1990s. There were allegations of collusion in providing clients with addresses of convenience outside the jurisdiction for the purposes of avoiding/evading tax liability. The hearings before the Public Affairs Committee of Dáil Éireann revealed much to the public about the inner workings of the banks. Senior officials were obliged to come and to explain their actions before public representatives. It was an exercise in transparency in which many of the banking community appeared to be devoid of experience. Banks were found to owe the Revenue Commissioners large sums of money in unpaid tax. Settlements followed. While public confidence was shaken in another of the country's major institutions, the process of bringing such an institution to face its responsibilities re-inforced the movement for greater openness in all areas of Irish life.

Other domestic factors also intervened in the 1980s and 1990s to create a crisis of credibility in institutions that were usually regarded to be beyond suspicion and certainly beyond the condoning of serious abuse and even corruption. A series of political scandals wounded temporarily the standing of the Irish political profession and of the probity of the civil service and of local government in Ireland. On balance, both politicians and civil servants have emerged as a body from a succession of public tribunals with their credibility intact. But the unscrupulousness of the few has created a major credibility crisis for the Irish political class.

The same has also applied to the public reaction to the role of civil servants and local officials. There was a crisis of credibility. But there was also the acknowledgement that the situation might have been far worse. The role of the Public Accounts Committee, mentioned above in connection with banking, helped in part to restore lost prestige to the profession of politics. The revelations of the different tribunals and the reports of Commissions, a number of which been chaired by Dr Miriam Hederman O'Brien, continued to underline the demand for reform.

The trust and confidence of the citizen in the capacity of the state and of other institutions to behave honestly, honourably and justly has been severely shaken by the series of revelations involving local government planning, the operations of the beef industry, the corruption and the alleged bribing of individuals in positions of responsibility. The touching belief that Ireland was cleaner than other countries in Western Europe, particularly those of the south of Europe, had no basis in fact. Besides, it was little comfort to citizens to learn that Ireland was not at the top of the European league table of countries where corruption abounded. The widespread presence of corruption in the operation of national government undermined public confidence in state institutions. It was very evident that the stronger the light directed on the Irish state and major Irish institutions, the more it appeared that closed government had simply provided the context in which undesirable practices grew up and had subverted high ethical standards.

Freedom of Information

The Freedom of Information Act was a partial, but incomplete, answer to arbitrariness in government. There are derogations and there are exceptions in its operation. There are institutions left outside the competence of the Act. Nevertheless, it is in my view a significant step forward. Its operations provide a daily challenge to the mind-set that holds that 'knowledge is power.' Whatever about the exceptions, the FOI has now been extended to many sectors of Irish life and the profundity of its impact has yet to be experienced in Irish society. It is becoming more and more difficult for any institution to claim that it has no obligations under the freedom of information culture that has taken root in the European Union.

Moreover, the Office of the Ombudsman has done most to make the citizen conscious of his/her rights when confronted by arbitrariness and arrogance. Together with their staff, the two holders of that office to date, Michael Mills and Kevin Murphy, have been responsible for initiating a silent – and sometimes not so silent – revolution on behalf of the Irish citizen. The annual reports of the office chronicle its record of achievement. In that regard, I was delighted to see victory recorded in one very important area.

On reaching a certain age, most of us unfortunately face the situation of trying to ensure that an elderly parent receives the best hospital or nursing home care possible and appropriate. There must have been tens of thousands of cases over the years of family members, in the corridor outside a ward where a parent was terminally ill, being asked about the joint income of all family members. This was asked in order to assess what maintenance would be provided in a nursing home by a health board.

As the eldest of eight, I faced such a question at a time when my mother was terminally ill. We were being asked to furnish the health board with the collective income of all eight children. In my unclear state of mind, I was convinced that the refusal to give this information would prevent a favourable decision being taken regarding maintenance in a nursing home. I inclined towards trying to give the information. One of my sisters was of a contrary opinion. She was angered by the insensitivity and by the intrusiveness of the question. But she was also of the view that there was no statutory entitlement to seek such information. It was neither seemly nor relevant in any determination to be made by the relevant health board of a decision regarding maintenance for a compliant and now terminally ill citizen.

The key word is, of course, 'citizen'. My mother had worked from the age of sixteen in the civil service between 1932 and 1946 when the marriage bar ended her career. She had also worked after the death of my father. But now she was a patient, apparently stripped of her rights as a citizen. She was a dependant. She had no rights in her own regard. The question of the degree of maintenance did not rest on her personal situation, it appeared, but on an assessment based on the cumulative income of her children. The question of selling her family home was also raised.

As I was to learn much later, the health board had no statutory entitlement to that information. My sister chose to give her income and refused to furnish the authorities with the details of the income of other members of the family. The distress that this caused in our case must have been multiplied thousands of times in other families right across the country – and for how many years?

A friend and colleague found himself in a similar situation some years later. But instead of being interviewed in the corridor of a hospital, he chose to correspond with the relevant health board. He set a trap. The arrogant official fell into it and the correspondence was sent off to the Ombudsman. It must have been one of a very large file of complaints received on the same topic over many years by that office. It never occurred to me in the difficult circumstances in which I found myself to send a letter of complaint to the Ombudsman. But fortunately others were clear-headed enough to do so. Thanks to the action of the Ombudsman's office the situation in which my family found itself will never again happen to another family in the Irish state.

Conclusion

Let me conclude by giving another example of a world that has been left behind – and that is very much for the better. I was working on a doctorate at the European University Institute, Florence, in 1976 on a topic relating to Ireland and Europe in the twentieth century. I wrote to the then Minister for Foreign Affairs, Dr Garret FitzGerald, in order to secure access to relevant departmental archives. Although there was no thirty-year rule governing access to official records, he gave me permission to see the relevant material for my study. I do not have the correspondence to hand as I am writing this chapter in the European University Institute some twenty-five years later.

Returning to Ireland by car, I arrived in Dublin to read the evening headlines that the coalition government had been defeated. But, as I had permission from the outgoing minister, I duly presented myself in the Four Courts where the Public Records Office was then situated. The courteous and helpful archivist gave me the departmental registers. Many files of the Department of External Affairs had been transferred in anticipation of the introduction of a National Archives Bill that, as it turned out, did not become law until 1986.

Having made a selection of the relevant files I ordered the most important. They were brought to the table where I was working in bundles wrapped in brown paper and tied with string. I took the first bundle and opened it with some nervousness. This was the first time a researcher would have been allowed officially to see the files of the Department of External Affairs. I undid the string and lifted up the first file. But before I could open it, the helpful and now very embarrassed archivist told me that I was not allowed to read the files. He explained that I had been allowed to *see* the files but not to *look at* the files. I don't remember the exact wording. But that was the import of the decision. The outgoing minister's letter was being observed literally. Yes, I did see the files. But the new interpretation was that I could not look at them. It was a very particular reading of Dr FitzGerald's letter. Who was the genius responsible for making that decision?

At this distance, the issue is now irrelevant. It was a temporary but not a permanent professional set back. There was some comfort in the fact that I did insist on *seeing* all the relevant files. I opened each parcel and held each file but, of course, God forbid, I did not turn the cover over to taste the forbidden fruit.

At the time there was considerable discomfort with the decision. I learned that when I was interviewed by a distinguished, fair-minded and highly embarrassed diplomat charged with the task of conveying the news to me that there would be no reprieve. A decade later, the then Secretary of the Department, Mr Seán Donlon, literally gave me the key to the 'safe' in Iveagh House where many of the most important historical files were kept and let me consult what I liked.

That decision gives a glimpse into the traditional school of closed administration. It was perhaps a last hurrah for a world that was coming under pressure to change. But it took a revolution to sweep the last vestiges of closed government away. The commitment of the former minister Eithne Fitzgerald to the task of bringing Freedom of Information onto the statute books made a significant difference to the content and timing of the passage of legislation. Many of the civil servants who made that freedom of information revolution possible 'subverted' the system from within. Many of their predecessors would not have been best pleased. But the democratic institutions of the state are the stronger for the ultimate 'betrayal' of the imported Westminster model of administration.

5

The Media in Ireland: A Distorted Vehicle for Political Communication?

Peter Feeney

Introduction

On 31 December 1999 there was a rash of newspaper and magazine articles and programmes on radio and television looking forward to the new millennium and predicting what was likely to happen. If one were to characterise the tone of the writings and broadcasts it would be that there was an air of optimism. The twentieth century, despite two world wars, a whole series of famines and huge environmental issues, was seen as a progression towards economic prosperity and democracy. The commentators and gurus exuded optimism as they predicted a century of progress with technological advance married to widespread increases in Western political values.

RTÉ broadcast in December 1999 a documentary called *2020 – Predicting the Future.* A group of eighteen academics and commentators from the sciences, arts, law, politics, journalism and economics were brought together for a weekend in the Tyrone Gutrie Centre in County Monaghan. They were given the task of predicting what the world would be like in twenty years time. The timescale was chosen because twenty years earlier RTÉ had broadcast a studio discussion in which experts had predicted what the world would be like in the year 2000. The weekend opened with a showing of the 1980 programme to the participants. After the showing people were encouraged to evaluate the accuracy of the predictions of the experts twenty years earlier. One commentator said that the only lesson he could take from the 1980 predictions was that predictions were dangerous and the wisest course would be to say very little. But his counsel was quickly forgotten and confident assertions were made about the next twenty years.

The experts predicted that the economic growth experienced in Ireland in the last decade of the twentieth century would continue. On the global front, there was some pessimism expressed that the inequalities in wealth between the developed and the underdeveloped worlds were so great that they might prove to be insuperable. However, the consensus that emerged over the weekend was that the world was on an inexorable path towards greater democracy and greater wealth. A minority held onto their pessimism, but they were swamped by the majority's optimism for the future.

What was missing from the weekend was a feeling that seems to be widespread in Irish society today. There is now an underlying cynicism towards political life amongst the public. This was not reflected in the group of academics and commentators in Monaghan. Perhaps the public at large, reeling from the revelations of the various tribunals into the activities of certain politicians in the last four decades, has the opinion that all politicians are in public life for what they can get out of it and that the politicians' commitment to the public good is a cloak hiding self-interest. The role of the media in encouraging and facilitating this viewpoint may well be contributing to a decline in the quality of public life and ultimately adversely affecting democratic practice in Ireland.

It is both easy and popular to be cynical about public life. It is harder and less popular to try and place in context the actual performance of public representatives and to compare their performance to their rhetoric. If the commentators did not share the public's cynicism could it be that they were less influenced by what was written and broadcast? As many of those gathered for the weekend came from the very same group of opinion makers that contributed to newspapers and radio and television programmes, there was the interesting possibility that they did not listen to or read their peers.

Within two years of those confident predictions, many of the underlying assumptions evident that weekend in County Monaghan have evaporated. There is no inevitable or inexorable path towards economic and political well-being. Economic growth is premised on factors that can disappear very quickly. But equally fragile are the underlying pillars of support for liberal democratic society. Events in New York, Washington and Pennsylvania and the subsequent military action in Afghanistan brought home to many people the inherent instability of political life and the unfounded optimism of the view that progress is inevitable.

The role of the media

One of the central pillars in democratic society is the mass media. At times of stability and relative confidence in the future, the importance of the mass media as vehicles for political communication is taken for granted. The assumption of progress embraces the media. The need to challenge the consensus, to explore alternative ideologies and policies and to debate alternative strategies and visions is neglected. In Ireland we have had a decade of unprecedented growth coupled with a sense that the major political issue that has dominated Ireland's history, the relationship with Great Britain, is moving towards resolution. Our political parties crowd the centre ground and compete, not with differing visions of the future, but with arguments that they would carry out essentially the same policies though in a more efficient manner.

Political communication is facilitated through the mass media. Politicians and aspirant politicians use newspapers, radio and television to communicate with the electorate. The battle for political influence and support takes place in print and on the airwaves. The era of political communication through mass public meetings has disappeared. Other means of communication, through clinics and door-to-door canvassing, are still important, but they only reach a small fraction of the electorate. So, there is a heavy dependency on access to and use of the mass media. It is therefore clearly very important that the media fulfil two functions. Firstly, that it is an efficient means of communications. This means that it is successful in reaching all the population. Secondly, that it provides an objective and fair vehicle for the transmission of information, debate and opinion. This latter function is at the heart of the role of the mass media in a democratic society. If the mass media is biased towards government or other vested interests it cannot fulfil this function properly.

The two major concerns relating to newspapers and broadcasting are plurality and diversity. Plurality is primarily an issue of ownership. Does the ownership of the mass media allow for a variety of views and opinions or is it tending towards a monopolistic position? Diversity is about content. Does the consumer find sufficient choice in newspapers and broadcasting? Are minority interests and viewpoints represented? Obviously these two concerns overlap. There is a third concern that applies particularly in a small country the size of Ireland. That third concern is foreign ownership. Many countries have laws that limit or control the degree of foreign ownership of newspapers and broadcasting organisations.[1] The nationality of ownership structures of the mass media is relevant if the local content of the media is diminished or if the editorial slant of the foreign-owned media reflects non-national concerns.

The technology of the print media and radio broadcasting continues to develop. But the pace of technological change does not undermine the inherent structures of newspapers, magazines and radio stations. New developments in web services, on-line publishing and digital audio broadcasting are all impacting on print and sound broadcasting, but that impact has had relatively little influence on editorial matters. The same cannot be said about television. The world of television has undergone huge change over the last two decades and that change has been driven primarily by technological innovation. Television today is an enormous industry with a growing tendency towards globalisation and the diminution of the powers of governments to regulate within national territories.

Television and politics

Viewing patterns

In 2000, RTÉ commissioned a survey by the Market Research Bureau of Ireland (MRBI) into its corporate image.[2] A thousand respondents were asked to name the source from which they derived most information on national affairs. RTÉ television came out as the most influential with 58 per cent saying that RTÉ television was their main source of news and inform-ation. Fourteen per cent said national newspapers, 10 per cent said RTÉ radio and 5 per cent said local radio stations. For local news, the local newspapers came out on top with 36 per cent and local radio stations second with 33 per cent. (If Dublin is excluded the figure for local radio increases to 43 per cent, making local radio the most important source of local news outside Dublin.)

When attention is focused on international affairs, RTÉ television is still the most influential with 44 per cent of respondents putting RTÉ television first. In homes with access to satellite television this figure goes down to 32 per cent. Nine per cent of respondents put UK television as the most influential, while 18 per cent put satellite television channels. National newspapers came in with 10 per cent, RTÉ radio with 6 per cent. What do these figures tell us? Clearly the dominance of television as the most effective medium of communication of news and information is clear.

These figures have to be interpreted with some caution, however. A survey commissioned by the European Commission Representation in Ireland into voting patterns at the 2001 Nice Treaty referendum showed respondents find-ing television only marginally more useful than radio or newspapers as a source of information on the issues in the Treaty.[3] It is difficult to reconcile the gap in relative influence between the various media in these two surveys. Perhaps the difference is explained by the fact that the emphasis in the Commission survey was on understanding a specific issue rather than a general understanding which was the focus of the MRBI research.

But what is clear is that television is the most influential medium. If this position continues, the very significant switch of viewers from Irish television to non-Irish television that has been taking place over the past decade carries the possibility that people's sources of information will move to non-Irish television companies. The implications for national debate and public life are clear. An obvious example would be the Irish public's attitude to, and understanding of, the arguments for the euro currency. The Irish media's under-standing of the euro differs significantly from that of the United Kingdom media, reflecting the differing economic and political interests of the two countries. If the Irish public had acquired its understanding of the euro from British sources, the debate in Ireland on joining the currency would have been skewed by considerations largely relevant only to people living in Britain.

AC Nielsen carries out a survey of television viewing patterns in Ireland on a daily basis. This service is funded by the television and advertising industries and is highly rep-utable. In the month of October 2001 Nielsen found that, in homes capable of receiving television channels from Ireland and the United Kingdom, 49 per cent to 50 per cent of the available audience were watching non-Irish channels between 18.00 and 23.30 in the evening.[4] The figure for non-Irish channel viewing has been increasing year by year as more and more homes in Ireland access non-Irish channels through the extension of cable and satellite delivered signals. This impacts on all kinds of programmes, including news and current affairs.

The loss of access of means of communication in political life may not be as sharp as these figures might suggest. Much of the programming available on all channels, whether Irish or non-Irish, is international in origin anyway. Whether the Irish viewing audience is watching an American-made series on an Irish channel or a non-Irish channel makes no differ-ence. What does count, however, is the numbers who stay with the non-Irish channel for news and information pro-gramming. Over the past decade, in common with all RTÉ programming, the amount of viewers watching the main news and current affairs programmes has declined. To give one example, the main RTÉ news, the 9 o'clock News, in November 1996 had an average viewership per night across the month of 673,000 viewers. Five years later in November 2001 the average viewership was 569,000. That is a loss of 104,000 viewers. If television news is a major vehicle for political communication, there are over 100,000 people lost in five years to that process.[5]

In comparison with other European countries the audience for news and current affairs viewing in Ireland is, despite the decline, still very healthy. The decline in viewership on RTÉ has not been as a result of the arrival of alternative news and current affairs on commercial television. TV3, the Republic of Ireland's first commercial television service, has gained a healthy 13 per cent share of the market. But its news and current affairs programmes have very low audience ratings.[6] The decline in the audience for RTÉ News is not explained either by the arrival of twenty-four hour news channels, CNN, Sky News and BBC News 24. Other than at times of heightened international tension their audience ratings are very small. Only Sky News is widely available in Ireland. The average audience share for Sky News in 2001 was 1.1 per cent in the peak viewing period, from 18.00 to 23.29 hours.

It is inevitable that, as greater choice becomes available through technological advances, the audience will be spread across a wider range of channels. Given the small size of the Irish market, it is highly likely that those channels will be predominantly non-Irish in origination. The implications for public life are clear. As more people switch from Irish channels to non-Irish channels, the ability of those in public life communicating through the most effective medium diminishes. We have witnessed a decline in voting in all forms of elections and some very low turnouts in referenda in Ireland over the past two decades.[7] This decline has reached a point at which the low number of people voting has begun to have adverse implications for the legitimacy of a very basic aspect of the democratic decision-making process. If television remains the primary source of information and if there is an increase in the numbers watching television that does not carry Irish content, or deal with national political issues, there is a real danger of a breakdown in political communication that could exacerbate an already worrying trend towards the de-politicisation of public life.

The decline in voting that has taken place over the past two decades is matched by a decline in participation in other political activities. All the major political parties acknowledge that active membership is in decline. Anecdotal evidence also suggests that the average age of members of political parties is increasing. The exceptions to this are the smaller parties such as Sinn Féin and the Green Party. Significantly, both these parties aspire to gather support from members of the public alienated by the mainstream political parties. It was most noticeable during the campaigning for and against the Nice Treaty in May 2001. The four largest parties, Fianna Fáil, Fine Gael, Labour and the Progressive Democrats, all called on their supporters to vote in favour of the Nice Treaty. Sinn Féin and the Green Party campaigned vigorously for the electorate to reject the Treaty. It became quite clear during the course of the campaign that the majority of people actively campaigning were calling for a rejection of the Treaty. Whether this was due to complacency in the larger parties, or was symptomatic of a trend towards the smaller parties who would characterise their appeal as anti-establishment, remains to be seen.

The success of those opposed to the Treaty is all the more significant when the support of the employers' organisations and the trade union movement for the Treaty is considered. Those advocating a rejection also point to what they perceived as support for the Treaty in the newspapers and in broadcasting. To convince the electorate to reject the Nice Treaty when so many parties and organisations were supporting it was a remarkable achievement.

The fact that the majority of the people who chose to vote in the Nice Treaty referendum went against the advice of the main political parties, the trade unions, the employers' organisations and the apparent support of the media has to raise questions about the efficacy of these organisations and groups in motivating people. Analysis carried out by Professor Richard Sinnott on the survey of voting behaviour in the referendum on the Nice Treaty suggests that the June 2001 result may be best understood by the relative maintenance of the vote of those generally opposed to strengthening of European institutions and integration, and the failure to vote of those who in the past had supported stronger European ties.[8] If this is the case, question marks have to be raised about the perceived level of influence that the media may have over public opinion.

An interesting statistic highlighted by Professor Sinnott is that the pollsters found that people who claimed to be more influenced by television were more likely to support the Nice Treaty while those who claimed to be more influenced by radio were more likely to be opposed to the Treaty. One possible explanation for this is that there is much more time available for comment and opinion on radio than on television, and therefore what influenced the voters was less to do with facts as presented in news and more to do with opinion and comment which were more readily available on radio.

Competition and ownership issues

Ownership of broadcasting organisations is an issue that has exercised the European Commission for a number of years. There is a tension between those who advocate minimum regulation and the free play of the market and those who believe the marketplace cannot deliver the diversity which is required. Often this tension is characterised as a struggle between commercial broadcasters and public service broadcasters. There is a fear that if the market is unregulated, amalgamation and multinational ownership will drive out choice and diminish diversity. Those advocating reduction in regulation argue that the dynamic of the marketplace and the opportunity to develop new technologies are inhibited by excessive regulation. The European Commissioner responsible for competition, Mario Monti, has argued for a *'nuanced' approach* in which a balance is struck between the need for regulation to ensure diversity and standards and the need to have a free market to allow for entrepreneurial opportunities to be exploited. He recognises that:

there will often be a valuable cultural objective in seeking to ensure high quality output. There may also be a
valuable political objective – fundamental to the health
of an open, democratic society – of ensuring media
plurality and a diversity of opinion within and across
media. A simple free market approach may not meet
these wider cultural and political aims.[9]

In the Republic of Ireland, RTÉ is funded through a combin-
ation of a broadcasting licence fee and advertising. TG4, the
Irish language service, is funded through direct exchequer
grants, programming provided by RTÉ and advertising
revenue. TV3 is funded exclusively by advertising revenue.
In addition, several television services not based in the
Republic of Ireland, but whose signal is available by satellite
or cable or from terrestrial networks, sell advertising in the
Irish market. For example, Sky Television, Channel 4 and
UTV all sell advertising in the Irish market. All these broadcasters make the Irish television advertising market extremely
competitive. The total advertising market for television in the
Republic was estimated in 2001 to be worth approximately
€190 million, with about €160 million of that figure being
spent on broadcasters based in the Republic.[10]

Looked at from the point of view of a concern regarding
effective political communication, the danger is that the
broadcasters who effectively do not carry Irish news and
current affairs content will take a large amount of audience
share away from those broadcasters who do. The other
danger is that the non-Irish broadcasters will take away
resources that could be used in the making of news and
information programming relevant to an Irish audience, and
use those resources either for their shareholders' dividends
or to make programming irrelevant to Irish concerns.

At present the other issue relevant in the Irish television
landscape is ownership. TV3 has moved from being predominantly Irish owned to being part of two multinational
broadcasting organisations. Some 90 per cent of TV3 is now
owned by CanWest Global Communications and by Granada.
CanWest is the largest media company in Canada with interests in television stations and newspapers in Canada,

Australia, New Zealand and Ireland. Granada owns seven regional television franchises in the United Kingdom and is the largest ITV company. Granada also holds 18 per cent of the shares of the Scottish Media Group which has become a player in the Irish local radio scene.

Currently, TV3 is obliged by the Broadcasting Commission of Ireland to carry 15 per cent home production including news and current affairs. In peak viewing time, almost the only Irish originated production on TV3 is its news programme. The obligation to carry 15 per cent Irish production, which they exceed as they carry 25 per cent home production, is achieved by carrying home-production outside of peak viewing when the available audience is small.[11] In summary, Irish production relevant to an Irish audience is largely confined to RTÉ schedules at present.

Radio

Those who listen to radio in Ireland listen almost exclusively to Irish-originated stations. The listenership figures for UK stations such as Radio 3, Radio 4 and Radio 5 Live are very small. The market is shared between local commercial radio stations who have 44 per cent of the listeners, RTÉ Radio 1 which has 26 per cent, 2FM which has 19 per cent and Today FM which has 8 per cent.[12] The amount of news and current affairs available on both local and national radio stations is large and accounts for a large percentage of all listening. All local stations have as a characteristic of their service strong local news content. The exception to this is Dublin where the two major licensed stations are predominantly music driven and pay little attention to local issues. This absence of local radio broadcasting in Dublin committed to providing local news and analysis has a detrimental effect on Dublin-based politicians who find the vehicle of local radio cut off to them. Dublin-based politicians are also disadvantaged by the absence of local newspapers in Dublin, though the extensive availability of free newspapers does compensate somewhat.

The national radio stations, especially RTÉ Radio 1, are major purveyors of news and information programming. The success of *The Last Word* on Today FM shows that enthusiasm for national news-driven programmes extends beyond RTÉ listenership. The 1988 Broadcasting Act, which regulated unlicensed local radio stations, has served well the goals of diversity and plurality in radio broadcasting. The first phase of establishing and maintaining the stations has passed successfully. The next phase, which is to oversee the fulfilment of promises and commitments made in the licence applications, has arrived and the Broadcasting Commission of Ireland (BCI), which regulates commercial broadcasting, is now faced with enforcing some of the promises made.

The BCI, which was previously called the Independent Radio and Television Commission (the IRTC), has to address ownership issues as well. The IRTC Guidelines imposed ownership restrictions to ensure that local radio stations were not amalgamated into too few ownership structures. In 2001, they loosened the restrictions. This enabled Ulster Television to take a majority stake in a company holding three local radio franchises in Cork. In another acquisition, in November 2001, Scottish Radio Holdings announced that they had completed the take-over of Today FM, the only commercial national radio franchise in Ireland. These two take-overs indicate the potential for a reduction in the diversity of ownership. The BCI has indicated that it does not regard local ownership and local content as synonymous.[13]

From a political communications perspective, radio broadcasting in Ireland continues to offer a range of services from a diversity of sources that make airtime available to those engaged in public life. The opportunity to engage in political debate and the delivery of news and opinion are well catered for. There has been little public criticism of the objectivity and impartiality of the services. Ownership issues, amalgamations of services and fulfilment of application promises are all likely to arise in the coming years. But overall, any assessment of radio broadcasting as a vehicle for political debate and news would have to be quite positive.

Newspapers

The Irish newspaper industry has served the public well over the decades since independence.[14] It has provided newspapers that take pride in the objectivity and accuracy of their content. A broadsheet mentality with a heavy emphasis on information and clearly delineated comment has prevailed. There has been little evidence of a decline into trivialisation or 'entertainment-driven' news. For years there was a balance, with one group of papers regarded as broadly supportive of Fianna Fáil, another supportive of Fine Gael and a third paper sympathetic to the old Unionist position. As these political distinctions evolved, the newspapers themselves became less identifiable politically.

The demise of the Irish Press Group did not cause the political imbalance that might have been expected. A process of distancing from party support was already well advanced, with Independent Newspapers less identified with Fine Gael and the *Irish Times* moving towards a paper supportive of liberal political issues. Today it is no longer possible to argue credibly that the Independent Newspaper Group supports Fine Gael. What can be discerned is an increasing acceptance of the need to understand and appreciate unionist understanding of nationalism. In addition the *Irish Examiner* has attempted to become a more national paper, by moving its focus away from Munster issues towards national issues.

What is challenging the Irish newspaper industry is competition from newspapers coming in from the United Kingdom. This is most evident in the Sunday market, but it is also an increasing cause of concern for the daily markets. The penetration is primarily a tabloid newspaper phenomenon. Other than the highly successful *Sunday World*, attempts at introducing a tabloid newspaper in the Republic of Ireland have floundered. British-based tabloid newspapers have filled that gap in the market. The three popular British tabloid newspapers, the *Sun*, the *Star* and the *Mirror*, all produce Irish editions with the majority of their editorial matter dealing with Irish public life.

The current circulation figures for morning newspapers in the Republic of Ireland are as follows: *Irish Independent* 168,000, *Irish Times* 119,000, *Irish Examiner* 64,000, *The Star* 97,000, the *Mirror* 90,000 and the *Sun* 112,000.[15] British broadsheets have a circulation of about 20,000 between them in the Republic.[16]

The net result of this extensive penetration of British newspapers into the Irish market raises concerns similar to those pertaining to television. Morning newspaper sales are currently around 670,000. Of these 351,000 are the three Irish daily broadsheets, the remaining 309,000 are either Irish editions of British papers or British papers. What this means is that only 53 per cent of newspapers read each morning in the Republic are Irish newspapers.[17] The 'loss' of almost half of daily newspaper readers to non-Irish sources, or to papers with limited Irish editorial content, raises the same questions about the efficacy of the mass media to provide the means of political communication necessary for the legitimacy of a democratic society.

This argument could be portrayed as a conflict between broadsheet and tabloid newspapers. But this is not the fundamental issue. The situation with regard to the newspaper content is not as critical for political communication as it is for television. Unlike the British television services which are viewed in the Republic, and which carry virtually no Irish news and analysis (except when Ireland impinges on the United Kingdom news), the majority of the British-owned newspapers selling in the Republic do carry a significant amount of Irish news and analysis. So the Irish tabloid newspaper reader is informed of Irish news, albeit in a somewhat contradictory form at times. The fundamental issue is the possible 'distortion' of the mass media in Ireland as a result of the non-Irish origin of such a high percentage of newspapers purchased in Ireland.[18] The market share taken up by non-Irish newspapers limits political communication and may also create an information deficit in relation to the level of knowledge and understanding necessary for informed political debate.

Conclusion

The similarities of market penetration in the newspaper industry and in television are striking. Those with a vested interest in the Irish newspaper and television industries may lobby the government to take steps to protect native production. But, in truth, there is really nothing governments can do. Any measures to assist Irish newspapers or television services would quickly run foul of European Commission regulations. In addition the circulation of newspapers and the viewing figures of television are market-driven. It is ultimately a challenge to journalists and production staff to create newspapers and television programmes which the public wants to read and to view.

Economies of scale issues contribute to the problems in Ireland. The production cost is not determined by the size of circulation or size of audience, but the revenue from circulation and viewing figures clearly is. If a significant proportion of the market is 'lost' to non-Irish newspapers and television stations, the resources to compete with newspapers and television services from larger neighbouring countries with greater resources will diminish, and the Irish media may experience a spiral of decline. If such an event were to happen the losers would not only be the media in Ireland. Irish political life would also suffer.

Notes

1 The USA, the United Kingdom, Australia, France and Italy all impose some restrictions on ownership of newspapers and broadcasting based on nationality.

2 *RTÉ Corporate Reputation 2000,* A Presentation to RTÉ by MRBI, October 2000

3 *Attitudes and Behaviour of the Irish Electorate in the Referendum on the Treaty of Nice,* carried out by Irish Marketing Surveys Limited, commissioned by European Commission Representation in Ireland (2001)

4 *A Weekly Report on Television Viewing,* AC Neilsen, October 2001. 3.6 million people have access to Irish originated television, but only 2.8 million people have access to UK and Irish

originated television. In this latter group, on average in October 2001 28 per cent of the available audience was watching RTE 1, 11 per cent TV3, 10 per cent Network 2 and 2 per cent TG4. If all households are included (i.e. including those only capable of receiving the Irish-originated channels) the figures are RTÉ 1: 35 per cent, TV3: 13.3 per cent, Network 2: 10.4 per cent, TG4: 2.4 per cent.

5 Figures provided by RTÉ's Audience Research Department.

6 According to the AC Nielsen ratings, in October 2001 the TV3 early evening news, *News @6.30*, averaged about 65,000 viewers, the RTÉ news running at the same time, *Six.One News*, averaged 480,000 viewers.

7 Richard Sinnott, *Irish Voters Decide: Voting Behaviour in Elections and Referendums since 1918* (Manchester University Press 1995), pp 82-89, discusses the declining turnout in Irish elections.

8 Richard Sinnott, Analysis of *Attitude and Behaviour of the Irish Electorate in the Referendum on the Treaty of Nice, op cit.*

9 Mario Monti, 'Active, but not activist', *Financial Times*, 27 November 2001

10 Figures for the television advertising market in the Republic of Ireland in 2001 suggest that the total market is worth approximately €150 million with RTÉ getting approximately €96 million, TV3 €26 million, TG4 €2 million. UTV it is estimated receives about €15 million from its Dublin sales operation, Channel 4 and Sky receive about €6 million each from the Irish market. (Figures are based on estimates from RTÉ's Sales and Marketing Division.)

11 Rick Hetherington, Managing Director and CEO of TV3, gave the figure of 25 per cent in a statement issued on 15 November 2001.

12 JNMR National Market Share of Listening Week Day 0700-1900, July 2000-June 2001

13 The Broadcasting Commission of Ireland, *Ownership and Control Policy Statement*, 2001

14 John Horgan, *Irish Media; A Critical History since 1922* (Routledge 2001), provides the best critique available of the current state of national newspapers and broadcasting in Ireland.

15 National Newspapers of Ireland circulation figures for January to June 2001

16 ABC, the Audit Bureau of Circulations figures for October 2001

17 The Irish edition of the *Star* is part owned by the Independent Newspaper Group and therefore cannot be classified exclusively as a United Kingdom paper.

18 About one third of all papers sold on Sundays are British, but as there is evidence of multiple purchases of papers by households on Sundays, it can be assumed that political communication is not distorted to the same degree as on week days.

6

Judicial Review

Sir Brian Kerr

Introduction

In this chapter I want to start by saying something about the foundations of judicial review and the debate that surrounds the question whether it has a single basis. I then would like to look at the exciting new dispensation that has come about by the incorporation of the European Convention on Human Rights and Fundamental Freedoms into the domestic law of the United Kingdom and examine a few recent judicial review decisions in Northern Ireland that have involved human rights issues.

Background

Judicial review is the main procedure for directly challenging the public decisions of public bodies. It is the most prominent element of contemporary administrative law. According to some commentators, the *fons et origo* of modern judicial review is the doctrine of *ultra vires*. Sir William Wade has described it as 'the central principle of administrative law'.[1] A lively debate rages about this claim, about which more presently. First, what is the doctrine of *ultra vires?* The traditional view is that in the judicial review context it has two aspects. Where a public body has been granted powers whether by Act of Parliament or other statutory instrument it must act within those powers. If it exceeds the conferred powers its decision will be quashed on what Lord Diplock in the *GCHQ* case[2] described as the ground of 'illegality'. In other words, the public authority will be condemned as having acted without legal authority.

The second aspect of the traditional view of the *ultra vires* rule relates to the manner in which an authority exercises its powers. It will be regarded as having acted *ultra vires* if, in the course of doing or deciding to do something that is *intra vires* – in the sense that the contemplated act is strictly speaking within its legal competence – it acts improperly or unreasonably. Examples of the improper or unreasonable exercise of a power include taking into account an irrelevant matter or failing to have regard to a factor that is relevant to the decision to be made. If the decision is one that no reasonable authority could have made, although it may (in the narrow sense) lie within the authority's legal powers, it will be quashed on what Lord Diplock described as the ground of 'irrationality'. Similarly, if the decision is infected by bad faith or if the authority has arrived at its decision without consulting those affected by it when an undertaking has been given that consultation would take place, then the decision will be quashed. The latter is an example of what Lord Diplock described as 'procedural impropriety'.

Professor Dawn Oliver in an article entitled 'Is the *Ultra Vires* Rule the Basis of Judicial Review?'[3] suggested that this second limb of the *ultra vires* doctrine rested on the interpretation of the instrument that granted the power. It was to be presumed that the giver of the power intended that the donee would act within the principles of good administration.

Ultra vires v abuse of power

And now the debate. Professor Oliver suggests that the notion that *ultra vires* is the single basis of judicial review is outmoded. Better, she says, that the court's supervisory jurisdiction be recognised as having a twofold function: first as a method of monitoring the competence of the authority to take the decision (*ultra vires* in the pure or traditional sense) and second as a check on the abuse of power. In an article first published in 1996, Dr Christopher Forsyth provides a robust defence of the orthodoxy of the traditional approach.

He proposes that the prime role of the *ultra vires* doctrine is to 'provide the necessary constitutional underpinning for the greater part (albeit not the whole) of judicial review'.[4] In support of his thesis, Dr Forsyth relied on the speech of Lord Browne-Wilkinson in *R v Lord President of the Privy Council, ex parte Page* [1993] AC 682, 701C-G:

> The fundamental principle [of judicial review] is that courts will intervene to ensure that the powers of public decision-making bodies are exercised lawfully. In all cases … this intervention … is based on the proposition that such powers have been conferred on the decision-maker on the underlying assumption that the powers are to be exercised only within the jurisdiction conferred, in accordance with fair procedures and, in a *Wednesbury* sense, reasonably. If the decision maker exercises his powers outside the jurisdiction conferred, in a manner which is procedurally irregular or is *Wednesbury* unreasonable, he is acting *ultra vires* his powers and therefore unlawfully.

The *Wednesbury* referred to in this passage is, of course, the celebrated case of *Associated Provincial Picture Houses v Wednesbury Corporation* [1948] 1 KB 223, which is popularly regarded as the source of the principle that a decision of a public authority may be challenged on the ground that it is so much in defiance of common sense or logic it must be condemned as perverse – hence the term *Wednesbury* unreasonableness.

Dr Forsyth argues that the doctrine of *ultra vires* is vital to the preservation of the separation of powers. Referring to an article by Sir John Laws[5] entitled 'Law and Democracy'[6] in which the author suggested that judges would oppose and strike down Acts of Parliament on substantive grounds because in the judicial estimation these Acts threatened the democratic order and fundamental rights, Dr Forsyth said:

> Were Parliament to enact such measures, we may be sure that the issues involved would be the subject of intense, passionate and doubtless vituperative debate in

Parliament and elsewhere. The measures, thoroughly bad though they might be, would enjoy the support of a majority of the elected representatives of the people and there would be large swathes of opinion in the country that supported the measures.

Any judge who struck down the legislation in these circumstances, not on some formal ground ... but on substantive grounds touching the merits of the measure would cast the judiciary into a political maelstrom from which it could not emerge unscathed. Even if judges were not removed from office, the judiciary would be perceived as politically motivated; its jurisdiction would be ousted in many cases; and, perhaps most gravely, appointments to the bench would be politicised.

This is strong stuff. It was, of course, written before the European Convention on Human Rights was incorporated into United Kingdom domestic law by the Human Rights Act, 1998. This provided judges with the opportunity to strike down subordinate legislation and even to declare that primary legislation was incompatible with the Convention where it was found to conflict with rights therein enshrined. A 'merits review' was inevitable under this new dispensation; it has been in place now for some eighteen months without the arrival of the appalling vista contemplated by Dr Forsyth. However, his opinions about the politicisation of judges provide a useful insight into the apprehensions of many about the 'onward march' of judicial review and its 'power hungry' judges.

A central theme of Dr Forsyth's thesis is that common law principles of administrative law such as *Wednesbury* have evolved with the implicit sanction of Parliament. They are therefore manifestations of the *ultra vires* rule. This is how he put it:

> ... the legislature is taken to have granted an *imprimatur* to the judges to develop the law in the particular area ... It is a commonplace for the legislature to give such evaluative tasks to the judiciary. This is inevitable – neither the legislature nor the executive can evaluate

everything ... an assumption that the judges have been given the task of so developing the law, within any limits that may be set by the legislature, seems entirely reasonable. And it implies no breach of the doctrine of *ultra vires*; in so developing the law the judges are doing what Parliament intended, or may reasonably be taken to have intended them to do.[7]

In a powerful riposte to this analysis, Sir John Laws said:

It is an elegant, but doomed, attempt to dress a fiction in the garb of reality. It confuses two propositions: (1) it is in actual fact the intention of the legislature that the judges should confine the powers of Parliament's delegates [such as ministers] by such doctrines as *Wednesbury* and so forth, and *for that reason only* they are authorised to do so, and (2) while the development of such doctrines is a function of the courts' free-standing constitutional role, it is open to Parliament at any time to intervene and curtail it. The first proposition is plainly false, and in reality is not supported by Forsyth. The second is plainly true, at least as long as the legislative supremacy of Parliament remains accepted.[8]

Sir John's analysis is surely to be preferred. The notion that the corpus of administrative law that has evolved over the past thirty-five years is somehow the unacknowledged offspring of an indulgent legislature carries the legal fiction too far. The development of the law on such subjects as substantive legitimate expectation could not be reconciled with a constitutional theory that the judges are the handmaidens of Parliament in the evolution of administrative law principles. The better view must be that the judges are the guardians of the common law and are responsible for its development and adjustment in keeping with contemporary mores and the requirements of modern society. This does not offend the fundamental constitutional order. The legislative supremacy of Parliament (including the power to alter or restrict the common law as declared by the judges) remains intact. The separation of powers is not threatened by a frank

acknowledgment that judges not only may but should develop the common law in the administrative law sphere as
in any other.[9]

I am an unashamed adherent of the Professor Oliver
school, *viz* that judicial review should not be forced into the
straitjacket of *ultra vires* but should find equal expression as
a check on the abuse of power. It may well be, however, as
Sir Robert Carnwath[10] has suggested, that 'there neither is
nor needs to be a single set of "foundations" for judicial
review ... that its proper place [is] as a form of procedure,
not a system of substantive law'.

The Human Rights Act, 1998

The dilemma that the *ultra vires* debate exposes is, of
course, a reflection of the circumstance that the United
Kingdom does not have a written constitution. But even that
truism now requires qualification. In the most important
constitutional development for centuries, the European
Convention on Human Rights and Fundamental Freedoms
was incorporated into the domestic law of the United
Kingdom on 2 October 2000.[11] The 'patriation' (as it is sometimes called) of the Convention was a long time coming,
especially if one recalls that the United Kingdom was one of
the prime movers behind the Convention and a party to it
since its inception. Now all common law principles and all
secondary legislation are subordinate to Convention rights. If
an item of delegated legislation is in conflict with a right
enshrined in the Convention it must yield to the Convention
right. Where, however, a court encounters primary legislation
which is in conflict with the Convention, it may not strike
down the legislation. Rather it is given a new tool: a declaration of incompatibility.[12] Furnished with such a declaration,
ministers have the power to make remedial orders to amend
the offending provision.[13]

Before the Human Rights Act, 1998, human rights had not
generally been part of the law of the United Kingdom. In a
number of cases it had been argued that failure to take
account of human rights rendered a decision irrational. This

approach was usually unavailing. When the argument was couched in terms of failure to give due consideration to the human rights dimension, it was not difficult for the decision-maker to have recourse to countervailing factors to justify the decision. Moreover, the courts steadfastly resisted the introduction of the Convention to domestic law 'by the back door'.[14]

This situation is radically altered by the 1998 Act. Now, once it is shown that an act, omission, decision or piece of subordinate legislation is incompatible with a Convention right, section 6 (1) of the Act provides that it is automatically to be treated as unlawful. This is important not only for the pre-eminence that it accords to human rights as expressed in the Convention but also in the juristic technique that is used to vindicate the particular right involved. Whereas previously, human rights – if they were relevant at all – could be considered only as a measure of the rationality of the decision under challenge, now incompatibility with Convention rights is a jurisdictional error of law. Section 6 (1) is in absolute terms. It is now unlawful for a public authority to act in a way that is incompatible with a Convention right. In this context public authorities include courts and tribunals and any person certain of whose functions are functions of a public nature.[15]

Judicial review and The European Convention

In this section I want to examine how the incorporation of the Convention into domestic law has altered the practice of judicial review in Northern Ireland and to review a small number of cases in which Convention rights have played a prominent part. The first (and so far the only) declaration of incompatibility that has been made under Section 4 of the 1998 Act was in relation to Section 62 of the Offences Against the Person Act, 1861.[16] It provided that attempting to commit buggery was an offence punishable with a maximum sentence of ten years' imprisonment. It was held that this provision was in breach of Article 8 of the Convention.[17] It provides:

1   Everyone has the right to respect for his private and family life, his home and his correspondence.

2   There shall be no interference by a public authority with the exercise of this right except such as is in accordance with the law and is necessary in a democratic society in the interests of national security, public safety or the economic well-being of the country, for the prevention of disorder or crime, for the protection of health or morals, or for the protection of the rights and freedoms of others.

Strasbourg jurisprudence[18] made clear that Article 8 protects consensual sexual behaviour between individuals. It was not argued that there was a pressing social need for the criminalisation of buggery between consenting adults performed in private. In effect, therefore, no justification under Article 8 (2) was canvassed. In the absence of a claim that the measure was necessary in a democratic society, a declaration of incompatibility was inevitable.

The Human Rights Act has also had a major impact on the law relating to inquests in Northern Ireland. In *Jordan v United Kingdom* [2001] ECHR 24746/94 the European Court of Human Rights dealt with a challenge by Hugh Jordan to the adequacy of the investigation afforded by an inquest that was due to take place into the death of his son. In November 1992, Pearse Jordan was shot three times in the back and killed in Belfast by officers of the Royal Ulster Constabulary. The applicant submitted that the inquest proceedings were flawed due to the limited scope of the inquiry, the lack of legal aid for relatives, the lack of advance disclosure to the family of inquest statements and the lack of compellability as a witness of the police officer who fired the shots. ECtHR held:

The obligation to protect the right to life under Art 2 of the Convention, read in conjunction with the state's general duty under Art 1 of the Convention to 'secure to everyone within [its] jurisdiction the rights and freedoms defined in [the] Convention', also required, by implication, that there was to be some form of effective official investigation when individuals have been killed as a result of the use of force. The essential purpose of such investigation was to secure the effective implementation of the domestic laws which protect the right to life and, in those cases involving state agents or bodies, to ensure their accountability for deaths occurring under their responsibility. The form of such an investigation could vary. However, whatever mode was employed, the authorities were to act of their own motion, once the matter has come to their attention. They could not leave it to the initiative of the next of kin either to lodge a formal complaint or to take responsibility for the conduct of any investigative procedures. For an investigation into alleged unlawful killing by state agents to have been effective, it was generally regarded as necessary for the persons responsible for and carrying out the investigation to be independent from those implicated in the events. The investigation was also to be effective in the sense that it was capable of leading to a determination of whether the force used in such cases was or was not justified in the circumstances and to the identification and punishment of those responsible. Any deficiency in the investigation which undermined its ability to establish the cause of death or the person or persons responsible risk falling foul of that standard. In the instant case, in so far as there was (i) a lack of independence of the police officers investigating the incident from the officers implicated in the incident; (ii) a lack of public scrutiny, and information to the victim's family, of the reasons for the decision of the DPP not to prosecute any police officer; (iii) no means of requiring that the police officer who shot PJ to attend the inquest as a witness; (iv) an absence of legal aid for the representation of the victim's family and non-disclosure of witness statements prior to their appearance at the inquest, prejudiced the ability of the applicant to participate in the inquest and contributed to long adjournments in the proceedings, and that the inquest proceedings did not commence promptly and were not pursued with reasonable expedition and that the inquest procedure did not allow any verdict or findings which could play an effective role in securing a prosecution in respect of any criminal offence which may have been disclosed, there had been a failure to comply with the procedural obligation imposed by Art 2 of the Convention and there had been a violation of that provision.

This decision has spawned a number of judicial review applications. In one of these Mr Jordan challenged the failure of the Lord Chancellor to introduce the necessary legislation to ensure that the inquest system in Northern Ireland complied with Article 2 of the European Convention on Human Rights. Article 2 provides:

1   Everyone's right to life shall be protected by law. No one shall be deprived of his life intentionally save in the execution of a sentence of a court following his conviction of a crime for which this penalty is provided by law.

2   Deprivation of life shall not be regarded as inflicted in contravention of this Article when it results from the use of force which is no more than absolutely necessary:
    (a) in defence of any person from unlawful violence
    (b) in order to effect a lawful arrest or to prevent the escape of a person lawfully detained
    (c) in action lawfully taken for the purpose of quelling a riot or insurrection.

In a series of decisions, the European Court of Human Rights has held that Article 2 affords procedural rights which include the requirement that there be an effective, adequate and official investigation into the death of a person killed by the use of lethal force. This procedural safeguard implicit in Article 2 comprehends the opportunity to examine the lawfulness of the force that caused the death of the deceased. One of the complaints of Mr Jordan was that the police sergeant who had fired the fatal shots was not a compellable witness. This was the effect of Rule 9 (2) of the Coroners

(Practice and Procedure) Rules (Northern Ireland) 1963, SR 1963/199 which provided that a person suspected of causing the death of the deceased was not obliged to give evidence at the inquest. ECtHR dealt with this argument in the following passage:

> In inquests in Northern Ireland, any person suspected of causing the death may not be compelled to give evidence (r 9(2) of the 1963 Coroners Rules, see para 68 above). In practice, in inquests involving the use of lethal force by members of the security forces in Northern Ireland, the police officers or soldiers concerned do not attend. Instead, written statements or transcripts of interviews are admitted in evidence. At the inquest in this case, Sergeant A informed the Coroner that he would not appear. He has therefore not been subject to examination concerning his account of events. The records of his two interviews with investigating police officers were made available to the Coroner instead (see paras 19 and 20 above). This does not enable any satisfactory assessment to be made of either his reliability or credibility on crucial factual issues. It detracts from the inquest's capacity to establish the facts immediately relevant to the death, in particular the lawfulness of the use of force and thereby to achieve one of the purposes required by Article 2 of the Convention (see also para 10 of the United Nations Principles on Extra-Legal Executions cited at para 90 above).

By the time the judicial review application challenging the Lord Chancellor's failure to introduce amending legislation came on for hearing, an amendment to Rule 9 (2) was imminent. It was therefore not appropriate to make a declaration that the Lord Chancellor was in default of his obligations in this respect. The court nevertheless held that the decision of ECtHR clearly called for the removal of the exemption in Rule 9 (2) and that a person who was suspected of having caused the death of the deceased should normally be required to give evidence at an inquest into that death where an assessment of his reliability or credibility was required.

This conclusion would not have been open to a judicial review court before the coming into force of the 1998 Act.

The case therefore provides an example of the court's capacity to examine the validity of an item of secondary legislation (the 1963 Rules) against the backdrop of the fundamental guarantees of the Convention. Had the Lord Chancellor not intimated his clear intention to remove the non-compellability provision, it is virtually certain that Rule 9 (2) would have been declared to be in conflict with Article 2 of the Convention. Its *legality* would therefore have been in issue. In so far as the inquest procedure purported to be an Article 2 compliant investigation, such items of secondary legislation and such directions as the Lord Chancellor might give that would affect the manner in which the inquest would be conducted, would be subject to scrutiny not only on traditional judicial review grounds but also as to their impact on the applicant's Article 2 rights.

A further judicial review application in relation to the same inquest challenged the coroner's statement that he intended to conduct the inquest according to existing (i.e. pre-incorporation) law and practice unless the Lord Chancellor had changed the law before the scheduled date for the opening of the inquest. It should be noted that the duty cast on the state to hold an Article 2 compliant investigation is not necessarily discharged by the holding of an inquest. The application for judicial review was refused, therefore, since it was not for the coroner to ensure that the inquest complied with the requirements of the Convention. It is implicit in the judgment, however, that if the inquest does not meet the necessary Article 2 standards the state will have to institute a form of inquiry freestanding of the inquest that will satisfy those requirements.[19] Indeed in an English case where an inquest had been held which was found not to have satisfied the requirements of Article 2, the Home Secretary was ordered to set up an inquiry into the circumstances of the death.[20] These cases illustrate the broadening of the courts' role in reviewing ministerial decisions, which has been brought about by the Human Rights Act. It is now open to judges to require ministers to take positive steps to ensure that an individual's Convention rights are protected.

Other examples of judicial review applications involving human rights issues include a case where the decision of a resident magistrate refusing an application for an adjournment was quashed where the defendant wished to have a particular counsel represent him;[21] a claim that a prisoner was entitled, by virtue of Article 6 of the Convention, to be legally represented on the hearing of a disciplinary charge within the prison;[22] whether it was a breach of a police officer's rights under Article 1 of the First Protocol to deny her the opportunity to apply for promotion because of her sickness record;[23] whether it was a breach of a prisoner's Article 8 rights to require his solicitor to be finger scanned and photographed before entering the prison for a legal visit;[24] and many others.

Conclusion

The incorporation of the Convention into domestic law has enriched and extended judicial review jurisprudence. It has not led, as the doomsayers predicted, to an avalanche of unmeritorious applications. Nor has it heralded aggrandisement by predatory judges of territory properly occupied by political decisions. Properly informed and conscientious public servants have nothing to fear from the Human Rights Act. If they observe the fundamental and easily absorbed precepts of the Convention, they have nothing to fear from the courts.

Notes

1 Wade and Forsyth, *Administrative Law* (8th ed., page 35)
2 *Council of Civil Service Unions v Minister for the Civil Service* [1985] AC 374, 411
3 [1987] Public Law 543
4 55 [1996] CLJ 122. Dr Forsyth is the joint author of Wade and Forsyth, *Administrative Law.*
5 Rt Hon Lord Justice Laws, a member of the English Court of Appeal

6 [1995] *Public Law* 72

7 55 [1996] CLJ 135

8 Illegality: The Problem of Jurisdiction, *Judicial Review* (London, 1997) 2nd edn.

9 An interesting commentary on the proper distribution of the respective roles for Parliament and the courts is provided by Sir Stephen Sedley in 'Human Rights: a Twenty-First Century Agenda' [1995] *PL* 386 where he refers to the 'bi-polar sovereignty of the Crown in Parliament and the Crown in its courts, to each of which the Crown's ministers are answerable – politically to Parliament, legally to the courts'.

10 Rt Hon Lord Justice Carnwath, a member of the English Court of Appeal

11 By the Human Rights Act, 1998

12 Section 4

13 Section 10

14 See, for instance, *R v Secretary of State for the Home Department* [1991] 1 AC 696

15 Section 6 (3)

16 This was amended in England and Wales by the Sexual Offences Act 1967.

17 *Re McR* [2002] NIQB 58

18 Principally *Dudgeon v United Kingdom* [1981] ECHR 7525/76 and *A. D. T. v. United Kingdom* [2000] ECHR 35765

19 Hugh Jordan (coroner) [2002] NIQB 19; Hugh Jordan (Lord Chancellor) [2002] NIQB 7

20 *The Queen (on the Application of Margaret Wright) v The Secretary of State for the Home Department* [2001] EWHC Admin. 520

21 *Re Doherty's application* [2001] NIQB 41

22 *Re Morgan's application* [2002] NIQB 1

23 *Re Shields' application* [2001] NIQB 46

24 *Re McCrory's application* [2001] NIQB 46

7

Governance in the Health Services

Ruth Barrington

Introduction

This chapter examines governance in the health services. Governance can be described as the processes, structures and procedures put in place to ensure that persons or organisations charged with responsibilities by government, shareholders or members carry out those responsibilities to the highest standards. A number of reports have identified serious shortcomings in governance in the health services – at clinical level, at agency level and in the system as a whole.[1] This chapter examines the challenges of governance at these three levels and suggests ways in which governance in the health services might be improved.

Clinical governance

The relationship between the medical profession and the health system has been tense since the middle of the nineteenth century. This was the time when the profession first became organised and government began to intervene to control disease, provide rudimentary services for the sick poor and regulate the practice of medicine. Political battles were fought in many countries in the twentieth century as governments with a social democratic disposition, seeking to replace the market in the provision of health services with a publicly-funded and organised system, came up against the determined resistance of the medical profession. In each country the outcome varied according to the relative strengths of the combatants and their allies. In the United Kingdom, government created a national health system which was free to all at the point of access, while in the United States government could achieve no more than a medical safety net for the poor and the elderly.

In Ireland, the attempt by government to create a national health service on the United Kingdom model in the late 1940s met the combined resistance of the medical profession and the Catholic Church, crystallising in opposition to the proposal of Minister Noel Browne to provide free medical care to all mothers, and to children up to the age of sixteen years. The minister resigned, the government fell and the affair provoked a major crisis of confidence in the republican ideals of the state.

The subsequent government took up the challenge to introduce free services for mothers and children and to extend entitlement to hospital care from the very poor to all but 15 per cent of the population. Their efforts were again met with the combined resistance of the medical profession and the Catholic hierarchy, but this time the political will prevailed. A mother and infant health service was introduced and access to hospital care widened under the Health Act, 1953.

The upheaval over health policy did, however, take its toll on the aspirations of successive governments to complete the building of a national health service on the UK model. By the early 1960s, official documents announced that the government did not accept the proposition that the state had a duty to provide unconditionally for all medical services free of cost for everyone.[2] Proposals to extend a free general practitioner service to the whole population were dropped and instead the Department of Health concentrated on improving the dispensary service for the poorest third of the population, developing a system first introduced in the 1850s. The remainder of the population continued to pay their general practitioner. In hospitals, publicly-funded care replaced the charitable treatment that was the norm in voluntary hospitals before the Health Act, 1953.

A scheme of subsidised, voluntary insurance was introduced in 1957 with the establishment of the Voluntary Health

Insurance Board to provide cover for the 15 per cent not covered by the Health Act, 1953 and those who were covered but who wished to be treated privately. The voluntary hospitals, unlike their UK equivalents, were not nationalised and successive governments pledged to protect their independence.

Another important outcome of the upheavals of the late 1940s and early 1950s was a strong demand by the medical profession for clinical independence, interpreted as the absence of supervision in professional matters. This demand, as we will see, was conceded and lies at the heart of many of the difficulties experienced with clinical governance.

What impact did these changes have on the relationship of the medical profession to the health system? The relationship continued to be an uneasy one, unlike the NHS where consultants and general practitioners quickly became the strongest defenders of the new system. General practitioners and hospital consultants have fought to maintain an independence within the health services. This presents major challenges to clinical governance.

This chapter, for reasons of space, focuses on clinical governance in relation to hospital consultants, but similar issues arise in relation to general practitioners. Hospital consultants have built on earlier concessions of the continuation of private practice, of clinical independence and of the independence of the voluntary hospitals, to secure a status in the health system that is quite unique. They have the status of public servants, not independent contractors like general practitioners, but their contract gives them many of the advantages of independent contractors.

The common contract

Up to 1979, there were two kinds of medical consultant working in the Irish health services. The majority were full-time, salaried employees of the health boards with pension rights. Their private practice was strictly limited. The other group of consultants were those attached to voluntary hospitals. They received no salary or pension entitlement but were entitled to a share of the income the hospital received for treating patients under the Health Acts. There was no limit to the amount of private practice they could undertake, either in the hospital or elsewhere.

Following pressure from Comhairle na nOspidéal, a statutory body charged with regulating consultant appointments, for a 'common' contract for consultants in both public and voluntary hospitals, a contract was agreed in 1979 while Charles Haughey was Minister for Health. The contract combined the most favourable terms of the public and voluntary contracts – a salary and pension for a 33-hour weekly commitment to public patients, paid sick leave, generous on-call and out-of-hour payments and unlimited entitlement to private practice both in the employing hospital and off-site.

In addition, the contract limits the role of the employing hospital or health board in disciplinary matters. If a chief executive considers that there is evidence of misconduct against a consultant, he or she must request the minister to set up a committee to remove the consultant. No other professional group in the health services has such a level of protection against dismissal by its employer.

What added to the uniqueness of the contract was the inclusion of the following definition of a medical consultant:

> A consultant is a registered medical practitioner in a hospital practice who, by reason of his (sic) training, skill and experience in a designated speciality, is consulted by other registered medical practitioners and undertakes full clinical responsibility for patients in his care, or that aspect of care on which he has been consulted, *without supervision in professional matters by any other person.* He will be a person of considerable professional capacity and personal integrity.[3] (author's italics)

The words in italics are of interest for a number of reasons. The contract appears to exclude not just the consultant's clinical practice from supervision but wider 'professional matters' such as how he or she spends contracted hours, the extent of private practice carried out, the resource implications of clinical decisions and his or her supervision of non-consultant hospital doctors. It could also be interpreted as precluding clinical audit of the consultant's practice by peer review or any divisional or clinical structure within the hospital in which a senior clinician could direct the work of the consultant. The effect of this clause in the contract is to give medical consultants the effective status of independent contractors within the health services.

The Deloitte and Touche report commented that 'the implications of the current role of the consultant, in addition to his (sic) clinical independence, means that once a patient and doctor come into contact, the relationship is a personal one between the patient and the doctor.'[4] How does one manage a major hospital with up to 130 consultants who have the effective status of independent contractors, entering into personal relationships with thousands of patients each year, committing tens of millions of euro in public resources for investigation and treatment? How does a hospital ensure that what happens during that personal relationship is always of the highest clinical and ethical standards? The consultant contract is a major reason why clinical governance in our hospital services is so difficult and why management of medical consultants presents such a challenge.

The overwhelming majority of medical consultants are people of professional capacity and personal integrity who give the highest quality service to their patients and their hospitals. But what is to be done about the minority who who fall below acceptable standards for the profession? The consultant contract makes it extremely difficult, time-consuming and often extremely expensive to act against an individual consultant who for one reason or another poses a threat to patients or to the reputation of a hospital. Action by hospital management against a consultant usually involves the minister, the Medical Council and often the High Court. Management is precluded from taking action against consultants that it would normally have a duty to take with other employees. An investigation by a chief executive into allegations of bullying against a consultant, for example, was halted in November 2001 by judicial review in the High Court on the grounds that the cumbersome disciplinary procedures in the common contract must be used to deal with such allegations.[5] Disciplinary action taken by the North Eastern Health Board in 2001 against a consultant on the grounds of misuse of the hospital resources, an action that was confirmed by the High Court, led to a prolonged breakdown in negotiations between the Irish Hospital Consultants Association and the Department of Health and Children over the health board's power to act in this way.

There appears to be no consensus between the profession and health service employers on the balance needed to protect the clinical independence of consultants on the one hand and to deal effectively with the minority of consultants who do not live up to the highest standards of the profession on the other. Nor is there agreement on management's legitimate right to manage the sum of consultant activity, to have systems of clinical governance in place and how that can best be reconciled with the clinical independence of the individual consultant. The *clinicians in management* initiative, introduced in the 1990s to encourage consultants to take greater responsibility for the management of clinical matters, has been a disappointment, with only a few hospitals actively involved in the scheme.[6]

Pressures are now building which indicate that clinical governance will be a key issue in coming years. The medical profession is coming under increasing scrutiny at home and abroad to justify its actions. It is likely that systems to promote good clinical practice will be seen to be as important to justifying good practice as record keeping has been up to now. The proposals of the Medical Council, published in 2002, to require medical practitioners to demonstrate clinical competence throughout their medical careers may also create a climate more favourable to better clinical governance.[7] Active management of risk in hospitals, required for insurance purposes, will also underpin the need for clinical governance. The positive moves towards the accreditation of the major academic hospitals, on the Canadian model, will involve an audit of systems and processes in the hospital, including clinical care.[8] Greater emphasis in hospitals on the quality of post-graduate, medical teaching, involving more formal professional and university accreditation, will also strengthen pressure for systems of clinical governance. In the light of these developments, there is an urgent need for changes to the consultant contract that reflect a better balance between clinical rights and responsibilities in the complex environment of a modern hospital and health system, changes that are in the long-term interest of the vast majority of consultants.

Governance of health agencies

Health agencies, in the context of this chapter, are those bodies established by the minister to carry out specialist functions nationally on behalf of the health system. They include the Food Safety Authority, the Irish Medicines Board and the Health Research Board. They can be distinguished from health boards that provide a range of health functions in a region or public hospitals that provide specialist functions on a local or regional basis.

Perhaps the greatest evidence of the failure of governance in the health services was the contamination of blood products by staff of the Blood Transfusion Service Board (BTSB) with the Hepatitis C virus and subsequent delays in identifying the source of the contamination. The Expert Group Report, the Bain Report and the report of the Finlay Tribunal identified the extent to which the BTSB had not adhered to its own standards and the degree to which its standards in the 1990s did not meet best international norms.[9] What is surprising is that little or no blame attached to the members of the board of the BTSB, although under legislation it is the board that has statutory responsibility for the organisation. The Finlay Tribunal in particular appeared to act on the assumption that the department, and by implication, the minister was responsible for the operation of the BTSB.

Nor did the experience lead to a fundamental rethink about the nature and composition of the boards of health agencies or their relationship with the minister and Department of

Health and Children. Such a rethink is overdue. What most have in common is that they carry out specialised health functions at national level, as distinct from general health services that are better delivered by health boards at regional or local level. Some, such as the Health Research Board (HRB), are established under the enabling provisions of the Health Corporate Bodies Act, 1961. Others, such as the Irish Medicines Board (IMB) and the Food Safety Authority, are established under separate acts of the Oireachtas.

In all cases, the minister appoints the members of the boards of the agencies, acting on behalf of the 'shareholders', the people of Ireland. His or her discretion to appoint members of his or her own choosing is limited in some cases by a requirement in the parent legislation that appointment is made following nomination by particular bodies or following election, in the case of the professional regulatory bodies. Despite these constraints, ministers have considerable discretion over who is appointed to the boards of health agencies and over who is appointed chair. Appointments have a strong political dimension, and in recent years, have been agreed beforehand by the parties in government.

The system of patronage appointments is defended by those who argue that it ensures that specialised agencies are responsive to the objectives of the government of the day, and that it is a way of representing the public interest. The converse argument is that the system of appointment (a) does not confer a democratic mandate, (b) does not guarantee that the persons appointed have a relevant expertise and, (c) since board membership is in most cases unremunerated, does not ensure that members will devote the necessary time to board business. The problem could be ameliorated by appointment of a higher proportion of members nominated by organisations with an interest in the activities of the relevant board, formal application and selection of potential members by an independent group (the procedure used to select members of the Human Rights Commission), the election of the chair by the other members of the board or, in the case of larger organisations, confirmation of appointment as chair by an Oireachtas committee.

There is considerable variation in the *modus operandi* of agencies. In some, board members are involved in operational matters, while others confine their involvement to strategic issues and formal accountability. The adoption of a corporate plan is considered core business of a board but only the more recently established organisations are legally required to engage in corporate planning.[10] The parent legislation of older organisations has not been updated to impose this obligation. There is no mention of a chief executive officer in some establishing legislation (HRB) while in others the chief executive officer is empowered to act on behalf of the board without, it appears, any formal delegation by the board (IMB).

The tendency to appoint all board members for the same period of time means that all members leave together with a consequent loss of continuity and expertise. The staggering of membership would reduce this loss and protect organisations from being without a board for a prolonged period of time, a debilitating condition that has happened too often in the past. There is a contrast in most organisations between their relative freedom to spend money on core activities with the requirement to have the consent of the minister to the creation of even the most junior posts in the organisation.

While financial audit has long been standard in state agencies, the concept of an administrative or business audit has not. A business audit would measure how well the organisation is achieving its objectives as set out in its corporate plan. Such an audit would help in establishing whether or not an agency was operating to the highest standards and act as an alarm system to identify problems at an early stage. It would reinforce the responsibility for corporate governance of the board of each agency. The audit would include a review of the specialised activity for which the board is responsible – funding research, regulating the use of medicines, approving adoptions, making blood products – as well as of the finance, human resource and organisational development systems that support the activity. In most cases there are international comparators that can be used as benchmarks of performance.

Every specialised agency should be required to subject itself to business audit once every five years and to adopt any recommendations made. The audit should be conducted by a review group of national and international experts, the membership of which would have to be agreed with the Department of Health and Children. Reports of such audits should be published, with a copy sent formally to the minister and the Oireachtas Committee on Health and Children.

The acceptance of this proposal would go some way towards reassuring the public that specialised health agencies are performing to the best international standards and that the responsibility of the minister, the department and the board of the agency for governance were being met, at least in relation to the specialised agencies. What about the governance of the health system as a whole?

Governance of the health system

The Commission on Health Funding was established in 1987 to recommend how best to fund the health services. In a neat side stepping of its terms of reference, it famously concluded that 'the solution to the problem facing the Irish Health Services does not lie primarily in the system of funding but rather in the way that services are planned, organised and delivered'.[11] Its analysis also missed the point in one important respect. The way the health system is funded provides a set of incentives that influences the planning, organisation and delivery of health services. The patterns of individual and organisational behaviour under an insurance-funded health system, for example, are quite different to those in a system funded from taxation. Organisations will behave differently in a system where taxation is raised centrally and redistributed compared with one in which the taxation is raised locally and spent locally. For these reasons, any analysis of the governance of the health system cannot ignore the method by which funding for health services is raised and the means by which it is distributed.

There is a tension right at the core of the health system which has given rise to much criticism and soul searching but which has never been properly diagnosed. The health boards were established under the Health Act, 1970, as regional organisations to which the health functions of local authorities were transferred. At the time, local taxation raised by the local authorities was contributing about half the cost of the services. This was a major reason why elected local authority representatives constituted the majority of members of a health board, as well as the need to emphasise the democratic legitimacy of the boards.

The membership of each board thus ensured a close link between decision making in relation to the development of health services and the accountability of elected represent-atives to justify increased taxation to their electorate. In 1974, in response to criticism of the burden of health spending on the local rates, the government decided to replace local authority funding with central taxation.

At a stroke the link between funding the development of health services regionally and locally and the democratic accountability of local politicians was broken. A whole new set of financial and political incentives was brought into play. The job of the local politicians, and by inference the boards, was to secure as much central funds for the development of health services in their region as they possibly could. The behaviour of health boards, so criticised in the Deloitte and Touche report – the competition between boards for resources and 'the distortion' of national strategies by local issues – is perfectly rational behaviour in the context of the incentives provided by the changes in the method of funding the health services.[12]

To over-simplify, what we have now is a system in which financial control is exercised centrally, responsibility for managing the health system is devolved to regional level and medical care is delivered through general practitioner surgeries and hospitals all over the country. In such a system, the financial, political and professional incentives work against one another and the result is a system that is not easily governed.

The debate about whether or not to provide radio-therapy facilities in the south east of the country illustrates the problem. The professionals involved are motivated by the desire to provide the best service they can for cancer patients in the south east, irrespective of cost. The case for radio-therapy has received strong support from politicians, including those on the South Eastern Health Board, who argue that the government should not discriminate against the people of the south east in funding the best cancer treatment available. Since the taxpayers of the south east will not be called upon to pay an additional tax to fund this service, other than what everyone in the country will have to pay, there are no unpleasant choices to make, no opportunity cost foregone.

The minister and his civil servants are then in the invidious position of reminding the professionals that a certain size population is required to justify such highly specialised and expensive facilities or suggesting that if local politicians want such an expensive resource they must forego other developments in the health system. The history of hospital development in this country over the past twenty-five years suggests that these arguments have not carried much weight.

What to do about it? The answer to date has been to tighten the financial screws on health boards to control their expenditure, the remedies varying from time to time. The Health Amendment Act, 1996 is perhaps the most sophisticated means that has been tried to reign in the spending ambitions of boards. Boards are obliged to adopt service plans that balance funding against activity each year. Bringing the board in on budget was made the personal responsibility of the chief executive officer, under the Act. Any over-spending is a first charge on expenditure of the board for the following year. While this may have assisted the department in controlling expenditure in the short term, it has done nothing to resolve the perverse incentives that are such a feature of our health system.

A growing school of thought lays the blame for the current governance problems in the health system at the foot of the health boards. There is criticism of the number of boards and of their political nature. The Deloitte and Touche report summarises the approach of those who believe that the problem is the political nature of the health boards:

We would suggest that at board level, there is a requirement for smaller tighter boards. In addition, there is a
need to change the political process such that the focus
of local political input is on a less representative basis,
i.e. representing the local population, and not on a
decision-making basis.[13]

We believe that the time is right for a detailed review
of the composition and role of health boards such that
an assessment can be made as to whether the health
board model is still the most appropriate means of
delivering service at a local level.[14]

One wonders what school of democratic political thought
would define the role of elected politicians as representing
the views but not taking decisions that affect the people who
elected them? Or what textbook of corporate governance
would justify board members whose function is to represent
the views of constituents but not to take decisions?

More crudely, Deloitte and Touche refer to an assessment
of alternative organisation structures for the delivery of services, on the basis that there are trusts in the United Kingdom
that are bigger than the entire Irish health system, without
defining what 'bigger' means.[15] Does 'bigger' refer to the
population served, the area covered, the range of functions
carried out or the budget of the trust? Providing a discrete set
of health services to a compact population in an English city
is a very different challenge to organising the wide range of
services that Irish health boards are responsible for in the
least densely populated country in Europe.

The criticisms of Deloitte and Touche are picked up in the
health strategy *Quality and Fairness – A Health System for
You*. The document promises an audit of organisational
structures and functions in the health system 'to ensure clear
lines of accountability and communication between each
part of the system, no overlap or duplication between organisations and a proper alignment of the structure as a whole
to the vision and objectives outlined in the Health Strategy.
The audit will consider the number and configuration of
existing health boards …'[16]

What is extraordinary is that no analysis has been made of
the financial incentives that give rise to the behaviour that is
perceived to be inimical to the implementation of national
strategies. Other health systems that are funded from taxation,
the Danish and the Swedish being examples, have managed
to encourage more responsible behaviour by citizens and
public representatives at local level. In those countries personal taxation is collected locally and local authorities are
responsible for all government business at local level. Local
representatives are accountable for both raising taxation and
spending wisely. Local authorities may vary the level of taxation, within limits agreed nationally, to fund developments
over and above the minimum level of service that must be
available to all.

Problems similar to those associated with the health
boards have been identified in many areas of Irish life, waste
management being an example, giving rise to a general lack
of responsibility and disregard for the public good both by
elected bodies and the citizens they represent. The phenomenon points to a general malaise in Irish government
that will not be solved by ever tighter financial controls on
local bodies or by removing elected representatives from
decision making, as proposed by the Deloitte and Touche
report[17] but may be ameliorated by more closely linking the
raising of taxation to the spending of it.

It is also disappointing that health boards have not been
given credit for the important contribution they have made
to the operation of the health services. The involvement of
elected public representatives gives health boards, and by
implication their actions, a democratic legitimacy that boards
with members appointed by political patronage, or a structure
in which decisions are taken by officials, could never have.
Bodies charged with delivering health services to a population
need this democratic legitimacy because of the nature of the
services they are delivering.

Encounters between citizens and the health service are by
nature highly personal, are mostly local and have a strong
ethical dimension. Most encounters are mediated by a professional who must assess the problem and recommend a

course of action appropriate to an individual or family. The Irish College of General Practitioners, for example, has estimated that there are 15 million consultations between patients and general practitioners each year.[18] The delivery of health care is not like providing an electricity or telephone service, where the only difference between households in the service they receive is the amount of electricity they use or the number of lines connected.

How health services are organised and delivered matters hugely to people for personal, social, ethical and economic reasons. Their delivery must be designed to suit local needs and aspirations. The decentralised nature of the business of health requires decentralised decision making. The highly political nature of health decision making requires a political means to resolve conflict and competing interests. Politics cannot be taken out of health, no matter how much some professionals, technocrats or management consultants would wish. Health boards provide a decentralised decision-making structure and a means to resolve conflict over health services in the interest of the public good.

Despite a perception to the contrary, health boards have taken extremely difficult decisions about the development of health services, decisions that would not have been accepted if taken by officials or by a national body. Any audit of the role of health boards that did not assess their ability to provide decentralised decision making, and to resolve conflict, would be grossly one-sided and detrimental to the long-term development of the health system.

What would be of great value would be an analysis of how to reconcile the bi-furcation of responsibility for delivery of health services and the funding of the health system. The challenge is to bring the financial and political incentives into line, as Scandinavian countries have done, to encourage responsible behaviour by citizens, statutory bodies and elected representatives, while at the same time guaranteeing a high quality of public service. There has been a rapid growth of government activity at regional level over the past thirty years but little or no co-ordination of this activity. Each region operates to its own boundaries and few have the statutory authority and democratic legitimacy of the health boards. What is required is a rationalisation of government activity at regional level, common regional boundaries, the direct election of public representatives to a multi-functional regional forum and the underpinning of responsibility for services with the decentralisation of existing taxation raising powers.

In the meantime, are there any steps that could be taken to more closely link responsibility for service delivery and the funding of the health services that would encourage greater responsibility in the system as a whole?

One step would be to have direct elections to health boards from a regional constituency, in place of the current local authority representatives. This would encourage representatives to have a wider, regional mandate while still protecting the democratic legitimacy of boards.

Second, the development of a resource allocation mechanism that would distribute health funding on a fair basis between health boards, as recommended by the Deloitte and Touche Report, would at least remove any perception of unfair treatment in funding by any board. It would be important that boards would agree to the formula to be used in allocating the available funding.

Third, a more rational system for allocating resources to health boards should be accompanied by the gradual introduction of financial flows between health boards for services provided for their population, for example, in hospitals outside the region. This would give health boards an incentive either to buy more services or provide them within the region, a choice they do not have at the moment.

Fourth, payments by the department 'on behalf of health boards' to various bodies, including the General Medical Services Payments Board, should cease and each board should be responsible for its own share of funding.

These steps would help to link financial and service responsibility more closely in health boards while protecting the decentralised decision-making structure and the political legitimacy of the system.

And of course any audit of the role of the health boards

should be informed by the need of citizens and of health professionals for a decentralised decision-making structure. It should also take into account that in a democratic society, the role of public representatives is to take decisions on behalf of the people who elected them and to be accountable to the same people for those decisions. They are not there, as the Deloitte and Touche Report suggests, simply to represent the views of their constituents.[19]

Conclusion

The health system faces major challenges relating to governance – at clinical level, in the specialist agencies and in relation to the system as a whole. The challenge under each heading is different but interconnected

The clinical challenge is largely a legacy of past decisions on guarantees of clinical independence that need to be reconciled with the demands of running a modern, responsive and accountable health system. There is an opportunity to address the issue in the context of the implementation of the commitments in the health strategy – *Quality and Fairness.*

The issue of governance of the specialist agencies is one to which little or no consistent thought has been given and which an updating of legal requirements and the introduction of a system of business audit could address.

The governance of the system as a whole presents a challenge of a different order. The analysis that has taken place to date of the problems of governance has failed to address the central issue of the perverse incentives that the division of responsibility for funding and delivering health services creates for health organisations and professionals working in the system. The system will not be better governed by further centralisation of responsibility for the delivery of health services or the reduction of the role of elected representatives. What is required is an alignment of responsibility for funding and delivery of health services. The highly personal and political nature of health services requires that this alignment take place at regional and local level.

Notes

1 *Report of Expert Group on The Blood Transfusion Service Board* (1995) (Hederman O'Brien Report); *Report of the Tribunal of Enquiry into the Blood Transfusion Service Board* (1997) (Finlay Report); *Blood Transfusion Service Board – Fact Finding and Analysis* (1995) Bain UK Inc (Bain Report); Deloitte and Touche (2002), *Value for Money Audit of the Health Services*, Dublin: Deloitte and Touche.

2 Barrington, R. (1987), *Health, Medicine and Politics in Ireland 1900-1970*, Dublin: Institute of Public Administration, p. 261

3 Quoted in Deloitte and Touche (2002), *op. cit.*, p. 177

4 ibid., p. 179

5 High Court, *O'Donoghue v. South Eastern Health Board*, 27 November 2001

6 Office for Health Management, *Clinicians in Management (3): A Review of the Initiative and Pointers to the Way Forward*, Discussion Paper No 3, November 2000

7 The Medical Council, *Competence Assurance Structures – An Agenda for Implementation*, March 2002, Dublin

8 *Quality and Fairness – A Health System for You* (2001), Department of Health and Children, p. 87

9 Report of Expert Group, *op. cit.*, Bain Report, *op.cit.* and Report of the Tribunal of Enquiry, *op. cit.*

10 Department of Finance, *Code of Practice for the Governance of State Bodies*, October 2001 (www.irlgov.ie/finance/Publications/otherpubs/code.htm)

11 *Report of the Commission on Health Funding* (1989), p. 15, para 245.

12 Deloitte and Touche, *op. cit.*, p. 128

13 ibid., p. 171

14 ibid., p. 173

15 ibid., p. 190

16 *Quality and Fairness, op. cit.*, p. 130

17 Deloitte and Touche, *op. cit.*, p. 171

18 Department of Health and Children (2001), *Primary Care – A New Direction*, Dublin: Stationery Office, p. 21

19 Deloitte and Touche, *op. cit.*, p. 171

8

Irish Universities:
A Look Ahead

Thomas N. Mitchell

Introduction

It is a special pleasure to contribute to a book in honour of Dr Miriam Hederman O'Brien, whose remarkable energy and varied talents have brought benefits to so many facets of Irish life. Her record of public service continued until recently in her role as Chancellor of the University of Limerick, and I thought it appropriate that this chapter should deal with a university theme. Irish universities are at a crossroads, as they adapt to the new conditions of the knowledge age and of the new Ireland, now an affluent society transformed by the economic boom of the 1990s. I would like to consider some of the issues that I believe are of immediate importance in university education and most likely to dominate the university debate in the years ahead.

Expansion and its consequences

The most dramatic change for universities everywhere over the past thirty years has been a relentless growth in demand, primarily the result of rising participation rates fuelled by a knowledge revolution that has made education the key to professional success. In Ireland the demand was further strengthened by the introduction of free secondary education in the 1960s and by a sharp increase in the birth rate between 1960 and 1980. As a result the numbers in third level rose from 23,000 in the mid-1960s to 123,000 in 2000, an increase in participation rates from 11 per cent to 52 per cent. In the university sector in the same period, the numbers grew from 17,000 to 63,000, increasing participation from 8 per cent to 23 per cent.

The expansion was necessary to meet the needs of a developing economy and the legitimate aspirations of young people to acquire a third-level education, and in many ways the developments in Irish education represent a great success story and one that has been rightly acclaimed in many parts of the world.

But such rapid and large-scale expansion inevitably brought problems. Only two new universities were created and they were, by necessity, initially modest in size. The five existing institutions had to absorb the bulk of the increased numbers, and most of them saw enrolments more than double in a twenty-year period. Such expansion would strain any system, but for the Irish universities the problems were exacerbated by the fact that, until the early 1990s, the growth was somewhat haphazard, a response to an upsurge in demand that required action but that was not controlled by any clear-cut state policy or set of targets. In the absence of planning there was an absence of adequate funding, and the economic conditions in the 1980s and early 1990s, which brought recurring recessions, made matters worse, forcing cutbacks rather than increases in government spending on universities.

The years of the economic boom helped, to some extent, to alleviate the capital crisis, and some imaginative and supportive programmes emerged from government and the Higher Education Authority. Structural funds, matching-fund schemes, tax incentive packages, programmes to deal with skills shortages, and, in particular, the Programme for Research in Third-Level Institutions – all of these led to significant capital investment in all the universities in the 1990s. Intensive fund-raising by the universities themselves greatly increased the level of spending.

But the bulk of the money was directed towards support-ing new activities and strategic development in particular areas, and it did not address the inadequacies of the central teaching and research facilities. On the contrary, the concentration on strategic issues and special initiatives and the diversion of capital resources to support them left less funding than ever available for general capital needs. Budgets even for maintenance and small capital projects continued to shrink.

As a result, while there are gleaming new buildings appearing on most campuses, the central infrastructural deficit remains, leaving most of the universities with over-crowded classrooms, libraries and laboratories, inadequate recreational and healthcare facilities, and substandard equip-ment and learning supports. Despite the welcome and substantial capital investments of the 1990s, the fact remains that the standard of the basic facilities of Irish universities falls far below international norms. This is obviously a serious and urgent problem, certain in the long run to affect standards and international competitiveness. Much has been done, but there is a long road ahead.

The great expansion brought still more serious problems in regard to recurrent funding. Recurrent grants took no spe-cific account of increases in numbers in the 1980s and early 1990s, and the bulk of the additional students brought no revenue to the universities except fees. The level of the state grant as a percentage of total budget began to decline. In Trinity College, for instance, the state grant in 1980 amounted to more than 80 per cent of the total budget. By 1990 it had dropped to less than 54 per cent. As in the case of capital fund-ing, additional recurrent income came into the universities in the 1990s, but once again the bulk of it was earmarked for special initiatives or for expansion of existing activities, while the core grant for central functions of teaching and research continued to decline. Between 1993 and 1998 over-all costs for the universities rose by 36 per cent, the core grant by only 25 per cent. The unit cost grew by 18 per cent, the core grant by only 4.5 per cent per student. At Trinity College the grant had fallen below 47 per cent of total budget by the year 2000.

Meantime there were additional burdens falling on this truncated income. New quality assurance procedures, access initiatives, new accounting requirements, new legislation, such as the Freedom of Information and Copyright Acts, were imposing large new administrative costs without adequate compensation. Many of the new initiatives, welcome and laudable though they were, and especially those involving capital developments, were not fully funded, and the shortfall had to be met by fundraising or by transfers from recurrent income. Similar transfers to meet capital costs were also often necessary because of the inadequacy of funding for routine maintenance and small capital projects.

The new programmes of the 1990s, especially those in research, were far-sighted, and are vital to the realisation of the national objective of creating a knowledge society. But their ultimate success and the success of the national goals for higher education will depend on maintaining universities that have strength at their core and broad-based capacity for excellence in teaching and scholarship. The low level of recurrent funding that now exists in Irish universities is a threat to that capacity. It has resulted in a sharp rise in staff/student ratios from 15:1 in 1980 to the current figure of 20:1, a figure far above the OECD average and a major obstacle to the interaction between student and scholar and to the active forms of learning that are indispensable to undergraduate education and that depend on low staff/student ratios and small-group teaching.

Underfunding has equally serious consequences for academics, increasing teaching loads, reducing teaching and administrative supports and diminishing the opportunities for research and professional advancement and fulfilment, all of which degrades the academic environment, inhibits achievement and is likely to lead to problems in hiring and to the loss of the most talented and mobile.

The capital and recurrent underfunding of Irish universities presents a complicated problem. The cost of maintaining a strong university sector has always been high and has escalated rapidly in recent decades. Universities are labour-intensive and use the services of highly talented and highly trained people. They require a wide array of elaborate facilities and equipment. The explosion of knowledge over the past half-century and the technological revolution have greatly expanded the range of their activities and the efficiency of their methods, but have also greatly expanded their costs. Governments around the world have difficulty meeting these costs; this problem is all the more acute in Ireland because of low investment in earlier periods. While higher levels of funding by the state are unavoidable, and certain to repay the investment, other courses of income need to be considered.

Most Irish universities are already engaged in fundraising from private sources. Efforts in this area will need to be intensified. Private giving to higher education has been a mainstay of many of the world's leading universities. It is time that it made a bigger contribution in Ireland, which now has a largely knowledge-driven economy heavily dependent on the intellectual capital represented by the universities and their graduates. The corporate sector and its leaders have a particular interest in preserving a flourishing university sector. They, most of all, need to invest in it.

The abolition of fees in the 1990s added greatly to the public burden of funding university education. The benefits went largely to well-to-do families, whose children continue to comprise the bulk of the population of our universities. Some of those who gained badly needed the relief, and no individual should be deprived in the knowledge age of a university education and no family should be subjected to unreasonable hardship because of either tuition or maintenance costs. But it seems reasonable and right to expect those who can afford it to make some contribution towards the high costs of a special benefit that brings lifelong personal and professional rewards. It is now time that the Irish government followed the lead of other developed countries and looked again at this whole issue.

A changing student body and new modes of learning

Looking to the future, the expansion of university services and of student numbers seems likely to continue, and the financial pressures certainly will not lessen.

Official forecasts would seem to belie this prediction, and there is a common view in some areas of government that, because of a sharp decrease now occurring in the school-leaving cohort, there will be a corresponding drop in the numbers entering university in the years ahead.

But the experience in the US over the past fifteen years urges caution about such conclusions. A decrease in the US in the college-age population in the early 1980s brought fears of an enrolment crisis that might close hundreds of third-level institutions. But, between 1980 and 1996, the numbers entering third level grew from twelve to fifteen million and the number of accredited colleges and universities grew from 3,000 to 3,500. Higher participation levels and increased adult enrolments were the reason.

The same factors will have a big influence on the university population in Ireland in the decade ahead. Current participation rates, at around 23 per cent, are well below those of many OECD countries, and are likely to keep rising, especially if there is any downturn in the job market for school leavers.

But whatever reduction there may be in the number of second-level graduates seeking entry to university, it will be more than offset by the need to cater for much larger numbers of mature students. At present Ireland ranks in the bottom third of OECD countries in the overall educational attainments of its working population. This is a result of the very low participation rates in higher education prior to the recent expansion. For example, in the age group 35-44, only 21 per cent have a third-level qualification and only 54 per cent have completed second level. In the broader span of working years, from 25-64, the numbers who have completed secondary education drop alarmingly to 28 per cent, and only 23 per cent have the benefit of a third-level education. In the age group 25-44, the group most likely to avail of second-chance education and most crucial to the capacity of the country's labour force, there are approximately 650,000 people who have no upper secondary education and 750,000 who have no third-level qualifications.

If Ireland is to equip its workforce adequately for an

economy that is demanding ever higher skills and educational qualifications, it must provide for mature student education on a scale not previously contemplated. This will require a major new public initiative and a cooperative effort between the state, third-level institutions and employers to create a range of supports and incentives that will encourage potential students to take on the significant burdens involved in resuming their educations. Better advisory services will be needed in companies and educational institutions along with more proactive forms of recruitment; financial barriers of all forms must be addressed; employers must encourage and facilitate the return to education by providing career breaks or flexible working hours and as much financial support as possible.

Many of the educational services involved will be provided outside the university sector, but a great many mature students will be seeking and will qualify for degree programmes, and the universities have an unavoidable responsibility to meet that demand. Other university systems are playing a central role in mature student education; it will have to be given a far higher priority in the Irish system than in the past.

This will bring change in the character of the student body and in the traditional structure of at least part of the undergraduate curriculum, as well as in methods of teaching. New access or bridging courses will be needed by some students to prepare them for a return to study and for university-level programmes. Since a high proportion of mature students will need to continue to work (and will be needed by their employers) while pursuing their studies, courses will have to be organised in a flexible, modular form and will have to be provided outside of regular working hours. Off-campus provision will need to supplement on-campus teaching, and this will require the full exploitation of new technologies, involving distance and online learning.

This raises the question of the role of the new technologies in the life of the traditional university and their impact on the future of higher education. The revolution in information technology has deprived universities of their privileged position as the greatest repositories of information and learning and as the primary centres for their diffusion through the face-to-face interaction of student and scholar in the lecture hall and laboratory and in small-group seminars and tutorials. New modes of communication via satellite, two-way video and online systems have made it possible to give students direct access in their homes or workplaces to an enormous range of information and to specialised and customised teaching packages along with expert interactive instruction and one-on-one tutoring.

This has brought a variety of new providers into higher education, offering a wide array of educational services by means of the new technologies. Some are for-profit companies, others are non-profit organisations backed by corporate associations seeking to ensure that particular educational services are available, while still others are partners with universities. They offer attractive advantages to the customer, ease of access, flexibility in scheduling, tailored content, reasonable fees. They have the benefit of low capital and operating costs and a global reach.

The new providers are here to stay, seem certain to expand their role in higher education and represent new, aggressive competition for universities. Some authoritative commentators, most notably Peter Drucker, believe that the new order of off-campus, technology-based learning is the way of the future, and that traditional universities with their massive capital requirements, inflexible calendars and time-tables and campus-centred methods of instruction and examining are fast becoming obsolete and financially unviable.

Such ideas represent an extreme view. Universities provide unique and multi-faceted services to modern, developed societies. They are reservoirs of expertise, the chief repositories of earlier knowledge and important custodians of our cultural and intellectual heritage. They bring together large concentrations of highly talented, expert people joined, as a community of scholars, in the pursuit of new knowledge and new ideas and in the communication of their knowledge and of the skills of investigation and reasoning that test and extend it. The synergies and insights produced by collegiality, collaboration and interdisciplinary interaction within universities and by an ethos that gives time and space to creativity and thrives on new ideas, create the ideal conditions that have led and continue to lead to the breakthroughs in knowledge that have done so much to improve the quality of human life.

Students who live in this milieu have the benefit not only of exposure to leading scholars but, in the words of von Humboldt, to scholarship itself. They also have the benefit of interaction with peers from diverse backgrounds and with diverse academic interests and of moving in an environment centred on learning and enquiry and geared towards social and intellectual development. The life of a university campus is a complex blend of social, cultural and intellectual linkages and influences that provide an educational experience that is comprehensive, unique, irreplaceable, and of inestimable value. It will endure.

But while the traditional universities provide services that are unique and that I believe will always be in high demand, they must keep reviewing their programmes and methods and must always be open to change. They cannot afford to delay in exploiting the benefits to teaching and learning provided by the advance in information technology. Nor can they afford to abandon to other providers the expanded range of possibilities in distance education made possible by the same technology.

Students must be given the fullest access to online sources of information, which means they must have their own computers or ready access to on-campus computer facilities. Instruction must extend beyond the lecture hall and seminar room and utilise the teaching potential of the internet. Training in content development and the uses of online learning must become part of the preparation for an academic career. Largescale investment in hardware, software, and training will be necessary, another daunting financial challenge for universities.

The Irish universities need to make clear policy decisions about their role in distance learning, particularly with reference to adult and postgraduate professional education. There is a burgeoning demand in both of these areas, and a large part of it will require, in both cases, part-time programmes delivered wholly or in part through the modern methods of distance learning.

I have already discussed the size and importance of the area of mature student education and the need for universities to take a proactive role in it. Postgraduate professional education is fast becoming an equally important societal need. It includes taught postgraduate degree courses, diplomas, certificates and specialised, unaccredited courses and seminars of varying duration. The growing demand for these various forms of continuing education is driven by the voracious appetite of the technological age for ever more advanced skills, by the fact that higher skills generally mean higher wages, by the pace of change in areas of specialised knowledge, which requires constant updating, by the instability and mobility within the professional job market, which leads to frequent changes of career and frequent need for new forms of expertise.

Universities in many countries, including Ireland, are currently providing a range of taught postgraduate, professionally-oriented degree courses, especially in areas such as engineering and management. Their involvement in the many other forms of postgraduate professional education is less extensive. But in Ireland, and to a great extent else-where, there is still a heavy dependence on campus-based, face-to-face methods of instruction. This is where change will come and where the new providers, the so-called uni-versities without walls, will exploit their technology-based model of distance learning.

There are serious questions here for the universities. To what degree should they seek to be the providers of postgraduate professional education and to develop the technology required for online delivery? The investment required will be high and will not be risk-free. The cost in time for both academic and administrative staff will also be high, which means that time and energy will be diverted from the core activities of undergraduate teaching and research and supervision of research students and given to ancillary activities less in tune with the central mission, activities that are service-oriented, narrowly vocational and market-driven.

Will this not obscure the key priorities of universities, lessen their control over what and how they teach and dilute the traditional values and purposes of university education? Should this work-related form of education not be left to specialist bodies geared to provide it?

It can be argued on the other side that universities have always adapted to the changing needs of society, and that radical innovations such as the introduction of professional faculties alongside the Arts (from the early intruders, Law, Medicine and Divinity, to the later even more unabashedly vocational faculties such as Engineering), did nothing, despite anguished cries from the purists, to damage the quality of university education. Postgraduate professional education can quite properly be seen as a vital service to modern economies, achieving the commendable effect of continuing to raise the level of knowledge and intellectual power of a society. It should therefore be regarded as a valuable adjunct to the other functions of universities, and a service that they have the expertise and systems to provide to the highest standard. It also provides a means of reaching out into the community and improving links with industry and the professions and countering the negative effects of the ivory tower image and the lingering belief that universities are unconcerned with the realities of everyday life and the practical needs of the marketplace. In addition, if properly managed it could be profitable and provide another stream of income to mitigate the chronic financial woes of higher education.

These are some of the arguments on both sides. They touch on fundamental issues. They need more extensive debate than they have yet received in Irish universities.

The changing face of research

The role of research in universities will be a critically important debate in Ireland in the coming years. The issue has a long history. In the nineteenth century Newman famously argued that a university is a place for the diffusion of knowledge rather that its advancement, a place to teach rather than to discover. The German tradition, represented most notably by Wilhelm von Humboldt, took a different view, arguing for the need to combine teaching and research in universities, each enriching the other. The American system, which distinguishes between research universities and teaching colleges, shows that the debate goes on.

Universities are, first and foremost, teaching institutions, but they teach at a level and with a purpose that make research or scholarship (by which I mean the work of critical enquiry that highly learned people do, using sophisticated investigative skills and methods of reasoning and analysis) a natural and necessary companion to the teaching function. It is research and the excitement of investigation and discovery that attracts the most able minds to academia and keeps them there. It is research and an ongoing active involvement in expanding the boundaries of a subject and confronting its unanswered questions that provide the mastery of their discipline required by university teachers. And it is the motivating power of research and the ideas and debates it engenders that provide the intellectual vibrancy and drive that are the bulwark of a university of the first rank.

These are the prerequisites of university education in its finest form. Universities teach the intellectually able at a sophisticated level, a task that goes far beyond the mere communication of advanced expertise. At the heart of a university education is the development of the mental powers and the skills of investigation, reasoning, and analysis. This can only be achieved by exposing students to what von Humboldt called scholarship itself, the process of critical enquiry and the hard and often painful thinking involved in asking the right questions and working one's way to reasoned and carefully tested answers.

This form of education can only flourish in a strong research environment, where teachers are scholars, driven by intellectual curiosity. Interaction with such enquiring minds, working at the forefronts of their discipline, is surely one of the greatest benefits of a university education and the means by which students acquire the mind-expanding skills that are the greatest source of creativity and innovation. In postgraduate education, which involves the training of researchers, teaching and research are even more closely linked. Training in research is a form of apprenticeship, its success directly linked to the quality of the research environment in which research students work.

The development of research and of a research ethos across all disciplines must therefore be a foremost priority of all universities that seek to be worthy of the name. On it will depend their intellectual calibre, their reputation, their capacity to attract talented students and staff, and the quality of their undergraduate and postgraduate education. For all these reasons, the development of research in the universities should also be a priority of the state and should receive adequate public support.

Until recently, the position of research in Irish universities was unfavourable in the extreme. It was not officially recognised as a function of universities until the Universities Act of 1997 and no special funding was provided for it other than a notional allocation in the block grant. The state's interest in research in general was low, and there seemed to be a clear sense that Ireland could not afford largescale investment in research and could not hope to compete internationally in this area. It languished near the bottom of the OECD table in terms of research investment.

The universities themselves also showed a lacklustre attitude. They proclaimed a commitment to research, lauded its value and rewarded research achievement. But planning and policy were largely absent and there were no structures to manage or monitor or promote it. A strong research ethos and dedication to scholarship persisted in Irish academic life and kept standards high, but researchers were left very much to their own devices, finding time and resources wherever they could. Many of them achieved remarkable things, but mainly by virtue of personal ability and initiative rather than institutional guidance or support.

But change came quickly and dramatically in the late 1990s, when the government, aware that the flourishing Irish economy was very heavily dependent on multinational knowledge-based industries, decided that, to safeguard long-term growth, the country needed to develop its own research capability to help build and sustain a strong indigenous base in the high-tech area. To that end it included in the National Development Plan for the years 2001-2006 more than €2.41 billion for research, of which €1.27 billion was earmarked for basic research.

The funding for basic research has generated three major initiatives. The first, a Programme for Research in Third-Level Institutions, administered by the Higher Education Authority under the overall management of the Department of Education and Science, is now in place and is providing capital funding, together with initial programme support, to enable third-level institutions to develop their strategic research goals and create centres of excellence in key areas, cooperating with each other to the greatest extent possible.

A second initiative has brought the establishment of two National Research Councils, one for the Humanities and Social Sciences, the other for Science, Engineering, and Technology. Both councils will be working to increase the pool of high-level researchers in Ireland by awarding prestigious postgraduate and postdoctoral fellowships, and they will also expand the most fundamental layer of research activity by supporting basic research of high merit across the range of disciplines.

The Research Council for the Humanities and Social Sciences is a particularly welcome development. From the time of Socrates, who is credited with drawing the search for truth down from the heavens and centering it on the nature of human beings and the principles that should govern their behaviour and social and political relations, research in the Humanities and Social Sciences has been an essential part of scholarly enquiry. It is the means to knowledge and appreciation of our past and our heritage and of the whole range of human creativity and intellectual achievement. It is also the means to a better management of our material resources and to a fuller understanding of the social, political and ethical principles compatible with the dignity of human beings and with human instincts and aspirations – principles that can lead to a resolution of the injustice and division that is the source of so much human misery. Support for research in these vital areas of knowledge is too often subordinated to the needs of science. Maintaining a balance is essential to the overall well-being of our society.

The third initiative is administered by a new Foundation, Science Foundation Ireland, under the aegis of the development agency, Forfás, and the Department of Enterprise, Trade and Employment. It has a more targeted purpose, to develop a strong research capability for Ireland in two areas with high potential for industrial development: Information Technology and Biotechnology. The Foundation has half of the additional funding for basic research, over €630 million, at its disposal.

These developments are transforming the world of research in Ireland and especially in the universities, but major issues remain to be addressed if the country is to build a true knowledge society and become a significant force in the international research community. The allocation for research in the current National Development Plan needs to be made permanent. Research is a long-term endeavour, requiring long-term planning and long-term funding commitments. There is also a major lacuna in the support for research in universities in that there is no source of funding that can provide even minimal levels of ongoing capital and recurrent research support across the range of disciplines, support that is essential if a broad research ethos is to be preserved and if new areas of strength are ever to emerge.

But the most controversial issue revolves around the question of how best to manage the state's investment in scientific research and achieve the advances in basic science that can provide the foundation stones for ongoing economic development. Some countries have decided that the best option is to concentrate research in separate institutes where clusters of scientists can focus exclusively on particular problems. Elsewhere, especially in the US, universities are being seen as the primary research resource. In other instances, research institutes have been located on university campuses and tightly integrated into the life of the university.

The arguments for concentrating basic research in universities seem to be gaining favour in many parts of the world.

University-based research enjoys first of all the enormous benefit of graduate students, whose contribution to the research process is attested by researchers everywhere. The point was forcibly made in a report by a US Presidential Advisory Committee in the 1950s, which stated that 'basic research and graduate education are the knotted core of American science and will grow stronger together or not at all'.

The wide range of disciplines represented in universities is also an important benefit in modern scientific research. Areas such as biotechnology rely heavily on the research resources of a number of disciplines such as engineering, chemistry, computation and medicine. These interdisciplinary resources are found only in universities. International collaboration, another essential aspect of many areas of research, is also found in greatest measure in universities, facilitated by the networking systems and mobility programmes that are now a normal part of the modern university.

But, perhaps most important of all, universities provide the ideal ambience for basic research. Their domain is the life of the mind; they operate in the world of ideas. They seek to encourage highly talented people to explore and test their ideas and hypotheses in an environment that values new thinking and supports people in pursuing it. Basic research thrives in such conditions, as is illustrated by the dominance of university researchers among Nobel Laureates in science.

The broad expertise and the facilities and favourable conditions for research that exist in universities cannot easily be reproduced elsewhere, and, in any event, few countries can afford the duplication without creating the risk that neither system will be adequately supported. In Ireland, where the overall research infrastructure is still, in many respects, rudimentary, such duplication would seem especially imprudent. There is the added problem that the country's pool of researchers is very limited and needs to be expanded as quickly as possible. In the short term, this will involve recruiting scientists from overseas, especially Irish graduates. They are most likely to come to institutions and colleagues that they know and to be attracted by the supports and benefits of a university environment.

It would seem, therefore, that the state's grand initiative in basic research could achieve the best results by developing the most significant existing research facilities in the country and locating the research in universities, whether within existing structures or in new centres integrated into the overall research activity of the university. Whatever happens, capital development will be necessary. That will take time, and decisions are needed so that the process can begin.

Conclusion

Irish higher education has come through an eventful epoch. It has been a time of great advances and it has brought a growing realisation that the country's greatest resource by far is its young people and the intellectual capital that they represent.

But dark clouds still hang on the horizon. The infrastructural deficiencies and general funding problems still linger, and the slow deterioration in teaching services and in the intellectual life and output of a university that inevitably results from chronic underfunding will eventually threaten the competitive position of Irish universities, if ways are not found to increase their income.

The expanding need for adult and continuing education and for easier and wider access to third-level programmes in general will have to be faced, not only by the state but by the universities themselves, who must be willing to redefine their role and redesign their systems. And universities will have to be proactive in managing and developing their research capability and in affirming their place as a primary source of new knowledge and innovation. The progress of the 1990s must not obscure the seriousness or urgency of the tasks that still remain.

9

The Social and Political Context of Taxation: Economic Policy in an Embedded Market

John Kay

Introduction

I first met Miriam Hederman O'Brien in 1980. She had just been appointed Chairman of the Commission on Taxation. I had recently become Director of the Institute for Fiscal Studies in London and we had completed our own inquiry into the basic principles underpinning the structure of taxation.

Miriam and I discussed together both the problems of investigation and the substantive issue of reform. We came to one radical conclusion – that it was time to look at the possibility of using expenditure as a tax base – which remains too radical for a government to adopt.

What was delightful about working with Miriam was her combination of fresh and genuine interest in ideas with an understanding of the social and political context within which any ideas had to be implemented. For many people who have not been involved in the determination of economic policy, that seems obvious. Yet for the best part of two decades, that insistence that market institutions must be embedded in the society in which they are found has been overwhelmed by an assertion that there are simple principles of economic policy which are universally applicable – a view of economic policy which I describe as the American business model.

That approach has now provoked its own reaction. In this chapter, I explain why there are no such universals, why economic institutions in general, and those of tax policy in particular, must be designed for the society of which they are part. And why Miriam's blend of constant intellectual inquiry with deep social and political wisdom provides the only basis on which economic policy can be determined.

One size does not fit all

In 1979, Margaret Thatcher became British Prime Minister and a little over a year later Ronald Reagan was elected President of the United States. These changes of government marked the reversal of a trend to greater government economic intervention and higher state spending. That trend had been characteristic of most of the twentieth century and had continued uninterrupted since the Second World War.

This change of direction was dramatically reinforced later in the decade by the collapse of the Soviet Empire in Eastern Europe and the disintegration of the Soviet Union itself. The fall of the Berlin Wall in 1989 symbolised Western victory in the cold war. One of the most extraordinary decades in the economic history of the world followed.

It was, above all, an American decade. As the Berlin Wall came down, the American political scientist Francis Fukuyama proclaimed 'the end of history'. Fukuyama's article in the *National Interest* extended into a best-selling book. For Fukuyama, the collapse of communism presaged an era of convergence on a common model of economic social and political organisation, based on liberal democracy and lightly regulated capitalism. The model bore, of course, a strong relationship to late twentieth-century America.

But globalisation and the American business model provoked inevitable reaction. The World Trade Organisation met in Seattle in November 1999. Rioters filled the streets and police were unable to prevent disruption to the conference, which ended in disarray. Every subsequent meeting of international economic and business leaders attracted crowds of demonstrators.

One such meeting is the annual World Economic Forum, held in the pretty ski resort of Davos in Switzerland. Its sessions in January 2000 were intended to be the culmination of the decade of American triumphalism. Bill Clinton flew in for the last such meeting of his presidency, to wave farewell to the business people who had gained so much during his tenure.

Yet it didn't quite work. The e-business sessions were still full to overflowing, but the reception given to Clinton and his economic adviser, Larry Summers, was somehow more muted. The party was ending. A few weeks later, the NASDAQ index reached its peak. Eighteen months later, it had lost three-quarters of its value. Most of the Internet businesses established in the mania failed. The collapse of the World Trade Center towers on September 11 2001 was, in its way, as potent a symbol as the collapse of the Berlin Wall twelve years earlier, as unalloyed in its tragedy as the other in its joy.

It marked, I hope and believe, the end of the 'end of history' – of faith that there is a universal model of how a market economy works, applicable to all countries and all times. There is, if not a clash, at least a competition, between economic systems: a world of many alternatives, each idiosyncratic and specific to its own particular time and location.

I believe that there are many common principles to be found among market economies, but that all markets necessarily operate within an elaborate social, political and cultural context: that all successful economic systems have evolved within a particular context: and that the context is far more than an add-on, an attempt to give ethical and political legitimacy to a fundamentally amoral market system. We need to learn to talk of the embedded market.

Indeed, without such a social, political and cultural context, market economies as we know them could not function. It is the failure to contextualise which causes us to be surprised when our standard models cannot be successfully transplanted to Russia or to Africa. The same failure to contextualise makes it difficult to understand the significantly but not wholly different routes to economic progress in Japan, Korea or Taiwan. And it is the same failure to contextualise that leaves us insufficiently sensitive to important nuances of geography – the differences that exist not only between the

United States and Europe, but the important differences that exist between the members of the European Union itself.

Fiscal neutrality

Nowhere has the transition in attitudes to market institutions which occurred after 1980 been more marked than in the acceptance of fiscal neutrality as a presumptive precept of tax policy. The fiscal equivalent of 'first do no harm' is the recognition that in general the tax system should not try to distinguish between desired and undesired activities. It should leave choices – between different goods and services, between investment and savings, between different types of investment and savings – as far as possible as they would be if there were no taxation imposed at all.

My own involvement in tax issues began in the mid 1970s. I can still remember the frosty reception I received when I talked of fiscal neutrality to a business audience soon after I became Director of the Institute for Fiscal Studies in 1979 and as Miriam began her work in Ireland. The concept was quickly dismissed as arcane and theoretical.

After my speech, a representative of an oil company explained that the objective of the North Sea oil tax regime should be to stimulate production. A representative of a mortgage bank explained how important it was that the tax system should be structured to encourage investment in owner occupied housing. A representative of a life assurance company explained that taxes must favour retirement saving. The tax system we had in Britain then was indeed designed, not necessarily well or effectively, to do all of these things.

Today, the term 'fiscal neutrality' has become a cliché. Much progress has been made across the world in the implementation of more neutral systems. Broadly based value added taxes have been introduced almost everywhere, and have largely taken over from selective excises as the principal generators of indirect tax revenue. It is now much less common to find elaborate discrimination between favoured and disfavoured activities within the structure of corporation tax.

Is this the result of the absorption into policy debate of underlying economic theory? Only to a limited degree. In truth, the results of that underlying economic theory are by no means clear cut. The main lesson of the extensive literature on the optimal structure of indirect taxation is that results are very sensitive to the particular specification of the underlying model. Perhaps the most robust finding is that taxation on intermediate goods should be avoided. That result has been relatively widely implemented in modern tax structures.

I suspect that many people involved in policy believe that the economic theory gives a stronger endorsement to fiscal neutrality than it does in fact – that the arguments that provide the intellectual underpinning of a generalised belief in free markets also rationalise uniformity in taxation. The policy conclusion may also reflect a looser association in the public mind between free market economies and an absence of paternalistic discrimination.

It is an association that has some rationale. The most powerful reason for prescribing fiscal neutrality is based less on our understanding of how markets work than on our lack of understanding of their functioning and an appreciation of their complexity. The strongest arguments for fiscal neutrality fall into two groups.

There is the force of general principle in resisting interest group pressures. Free trade is not an optimal regime in many circumstances – the economic arguments are complex, and there are many instances where departures from free trade would have advantages. But we also know that to abandon a presumption of free trade is to ensure the attentions of a queue of lobbyists stretching all the way round Capitol Hill. And the same is true of fiscal neutrality. Not to have such a presumption requires us to listen to the oil company, the mortgage lenders, the life assurance companies.

The second group of arguments recognises the unintended consequences of departures from neutrality and the difficulty of giving legal content to apparently common sense distinctions. Where do we draw the line between fresh food (subject to a reduced rate of value added tax in Europe) and restaurant meals (taxed at the standard rate)?

In Britain, the line is drawn through a pie shop. Cold pies are fresh food, but hot pies to take away are meals. But what of a pie shop that is so busy at lunch time that the pies, fresh baked from the oven, require no further heating to release their full flavour and aroma? It is better for the legitimacy of a tax system that the courts are not involved in reviewing these issues, but unfortunately that has not proved to be the case.

The purely economic argument for fiscal neutrality fails, or at least demands particular assumptions which are not necessarily fulfilled. The two arguments which I believe succeed are not purely economic arguments. One reflects the public choice nature of modern political discourse – the importance of simple, credible targets in economic management, an issue more generally recognised in macroeconomic than microeconomic policy. The other identifies the common sources of distortion and complexity in tax structures.

Neither are purely economic arguments. Yet they are arguments which would only be framed and presented through economic analysis. They reflect not so much economic theory as an economic view of the world. They are a product of the essential embeddedness of modern economic institutions.

Tax and benefit policies

Benefits, including retirement benefits, are the largest component of government budgets in all rich states, and they are also the principal explanation of differences between countries in their overall levels of public expenditure. This is the most important of many reasons why tax and benefit policies need to be considered together. The twenty years to the mid 1970s saw a rapid increase in expenditure on benefits throughout the developed world. This rise was more or less halted in the final two decades of the century. This check to the growth of social security spending is often attributed to a recognition that European levels of benefit expenditure were unaffordable.

But this claim is hard to take seriously. There is little evidence of significant effects on either the level or growth of

GDP associated with differences in the overall levels of taxation or of benefit expenditure among already rich states. And the shares of spending in GDP at which these levels of spending stabilised vary substantially across European countries.

The real cap on taxation, spending and benefit levels was proximately political, not economic. In California, the limits were famously enshrined in a taxpayers' revolt: a state wide vote on 'Proposition 13' imposed overall limits on state spending. More generally, limits to taxation and expenditure levels were set by politicians' perceptions of what they needed to do to secure election or re-election.

Although there were similarities in the outcomes on the two sides of the Atlantic, there were major differences in the way these outcomes came about. England and the United States, as we know, are two countries divided by a common language. In the United States, 'Social Security' refers to benefits paid to the elderly and the term 'welfare' is applied to benefits paid to people of working age. In British English, the term social security is used for benefits of both kinds.

This is not simply a semantic question. The difference in the use of words is the product of a difference between a European benefit structure rooted in the Bismarckian concept of social insurance and the American perception of welfare as a safety net. In one model, social security is an expression of communal solidarity: in the other, welfare is an institutionalisation of principles of charity.

Of course, both these motives and both these types of benefit have existed in both continents. In Europe today, social insurance and welfare are found side by side. Through social insurance, we provide contingent benefits many of which are received by individuals who are not in any sense poor. Through welfare, we offer a means-tested safety net for low-income households.

In the immediate post-war period, the proportion of elderly people in the population grew rapidly, offsetting the fall in the numbers unemployed: but unemployment levels bottomed out in the late 1960s and have since demanded a growing proportion of benefit expenditure and taxation revenues. However, the most rapidly expanding groups of benefit recipients throughout have been single parents and the semi-retired – older people, no longer in full time employment, often in receipt of sickness or disability benefit, but less deserving, in the eyes of many taxpayers, than the retired or those genuinely seeking work and failing to find it.

Concerns about both costs and beneficiaries have imposed strain on the solidarity underpinning benefit provision. This has been aggravated in turn by attempts to rephrase historic arguments for benefit provision in terms of individual rights. The concept of economic rights is a post-war invention, and in its policy implications is problematic. What establishes limits – upper or lower – to the level of benefits to which economic rights convey entitlement? This increased assertion of welfare rights has not been matched by any willingness to accept the corresponding cost obligations. The assertion that social security – in its European sense – is a right, has probably led ultimately to less, not more, being spent on benefit provision.

There are two routes ahead for European benefit systems. One – the one which has been widely advocated and often asserted to be inevitable in the last two decades – can be briefly described as Americanisation, a move to individual provision of retirement benefit, accompanied by a welfare model of means-tested benefits for those who are victims of other contingencies. The second is a revived concept of social solidarity.

The interrelationship between tax and benefits

The choice is most obvious at the interface between tax and benefits. Before the Second World War, taxpayers and benefit recipients were generally disjoint groups. Indeed a substantial proportion of the population could expect to pay in tax only excise duties on a few selected commodities and would receive no cash benefits from the state.

But throughout the post-war era, the vast majority of European households have found themselves both direct taxpayers and benefit recipients. This seems illogical. Should we not integrate the two parts of the household's relationship with the state? Many schemes have been put forward with this objective. These schemes are generally entitled social dividend, or citizen's income, when put forward from the political left, and negative income tax when put forward from the political right.

Despite the radical differences in terminology, the proposals are in all essentials the same, and do not work in pure form. Neither a scheme of purely contingent benefits (social insurance) nor a system of pure means-tested benefits (welfare) can achieve high levels of social support without very high marginal tax rates. An efficient mechanism, i.e. one which achieves the best balance between social support and marginal tax rates, necessarily includes both contingent and means-tested components.

More complex mechanisms are therefore required. It is now over fifteen years since I was engaged in perhaps the most extensively articulated attempt to develop an integrated tax and benefit structure for the UK. The question we posed was the following: 'Take as given the stated and inferred intentions of the tax and benefit system, in terms of the distribution of income net of tax and benefits. What are the best mechanisms for bringing about that result?' The criteria of judging best were (a) low marginal tax rates, especially where labour supply was likely to be sensitive to marginal tax rates, (b) maximum efficiency of administration, itself judged in terms of low costs and its effectiveness in reaching intended beneficiaries.

My view today is that this is an inappropriate way of framing the issue. The mistake is to judge distributional outcomes purely by final states, without regard to the processes which give rise to them. In terms of the dilemma posed above – the choice between the rights-based, positive freedom view of distributional equity, and the solidtaristic one, it falls firmly into the rights-based camp. Equity is judged by reference to the distribution of incomes net of tax and benefits, and the question of how such equity is to be achieved is seen as essentially a technical problem.

But from an embedded market perspective, it is not a purely technical problem. That is why the term exclusion is increasingly used when once we would have talked of poverty. Exclusion is an inability to participate in important aspects of society, the experience of exclusion which makes sense of relative concepts of poverty in a modern Europe where affluence is widespread. It has always been difficult to explain what we mean when we say someone who can only just afford satellite television is poor in a world in which most people do not even have electric power.

These western households are not poor, but they do risk exclusion. And inclusion and exclusion are products of the processes of the market economy, not just its outcomes. That emphasis on process rather than final states changes many aspects of the way we think about policy. We respond to the problem of unemployment because we recognise an obligation to help affected individuals to find a job, or if this is not possible to enable them to experience unemployment with dignity. These are fundamentally different objectives from the objective of the payment of compensation to those who are unemployed.

When we think in these terms, we find nothing paradoxical about individuals receiving benefits – by virtue of experiencing some contingency, such as redundancy, disability or parental responsibilities – which confers benefit entitlement, and still being substantial taxpayers. Association with other members of the affected group, and of the relationship between this group and society as a whole, is as important as the distribution of final incomes which the fiscal system seeks to bring about.

Income and expenditure taxation

The balance between income and expenditure taxation continues to be a primary issue in tax policy. There is some similarity between the issues here and those relating to fiscal neutrality. The result of numerous attempts to build models of the optimal tax rate on savings is indecisive. Again, the conclusions of such models appear to be sensitive to their exact specifications. The informal arguments which criticise 'the double taxation of savings', or which (correctly) note the distortions which arise if savings are taxed, cannot be easily translated into rigorous arguments, because some distorting taxes are inevitable in an economy in which lump sum taxation is not possible.

The more powerful arguments for expenditure taxation have always been based on the complexities which arise from the difficulties of translating a concept of income into an operational measure which can be administered by tax inspectors. The professional economist's favoured definition of income continues to be the famous dictum of Sir John Hicks: 'income is what a man (*sic*) can consume during a week and still expect to be as well off at the end as at the beginning.' It is immediately apparent why this is unhelpful for the taxman: how does he cope with the words 'expect' and 'well off'? The measurement of income is fundamentally subjective, and presupposes a capacity to determine asset values. Directly and indirectly, these problems have preoccupied tax judges and tax collectors for the two centuries we have had income tax – and are responsible for a large part of the complexity that universally characterises tax codes.

The calculation of liability to expenditure taxation is related to transactions, rather than to concepts which use primary data as an input into subjective calculation. The most important development in tax policy worldwide in the last forty years has been the adoption and extension of a broad-based expenditure tax – VAT – in every major Western country outside the United States. The cause of the shift is the relative ease of monitoring a transactions base. And the advance of information technology has steadily reduced the cost of implementing tax systems whose collection activities require extensive computation, while the cost of implementing systems that require extensive judgement and assessment has steadily increased.

The same phenomenon is at work within the income tax system. Within the personal income tax system there has been a general shift from comprehensive income to earnings: lower taxes on capital income relative to taxes on earned income, more concessions towards savings, a rise in the proportion of (earnings-based) social security contributions as a share of total tax revenues. In terms of its contribution to total tax revenues, corporation taxes have generally accounted for a declining share, although any clarity in the picture is disguised by fluctuations in the overall share of corporate profits in national income.

Overall, the dominant influence on the development of the tax system has been the interaction of ideas with technological and institutional change. And the advocates of expenditure taxation – including Miriam and myself – have lost many battles but are winning the war. The prospects of a root and branch reform leading to a substitution of a formal expenditure tax for all or part of the current income tax are certainly no better today than they were one, two, or three years ago. But the overall shape of the income tax structure continues to evolve in ways which leave it looking more and more like an expenditure tax and less and less like a comprehensive income tax.

Taxation in an embedded market

The theory of optimal taxation has been one of the key developments in the economies of public finance in recent decades. But such a theory cannot provide any direct policy prescriptions. There is no economic theory, and no possibility of economic theory, that can prove – or disprove – the case for fiscal neutrality, determine the optimal structure and social benefits, or demonstrate the superiority of expenditure taxation over income taxation.

The purpose of economic models in these fields is not to make policy recommendations, but to force us to understand better the structure of economic arguments, to appreciate more clearly the costs of distortions to the pattern of economic activity, to understand more fully the trade-offs between redistribution and incentive, and the differences between average and marginal rates of taxation, and to examine the ways in which the quantity and direction of savings and investment can be influenced by the tax structure.

However, the framing of policy demands that these arguments be integrated into the context within which they are to be implemented. In this chapter, I have given three examples of how this interaction occurs. The case for fiscal neutrality rests, above all, on the political advantages of a coherent, defensible position against political lobbies. The inter-relationship between tax and benefits is necessarily the product of the social philosophy which underpins these structures. And the choice between income and expenditure taxation is influenced by the changes in technology which have transformed the relative costs of comprehensive record keeping and subjective assessment.

It is for these reasons that the making of tax policy always demands a wide-ranging and sophisticated appreciation of the culture within which such policy is to be implemented. Policy recommendations, like the market economy itself, must always be embedded in the society of which they are part.

10

Homelessness and Exclusion

Peter McVerry

Introduction

Those who say that people who are homeless are homeless by choice are quite correct – but it is a choice that someone else has made!

When the Minister for Finance was receiving a lot of criticism over the cost of accommodating the rapidly growing number of asylum seekers, he replied, without apparently realising the irony of his remark: 'Well, what do you want us to do? Let them live on the streets?' When available accommodation seemed to be inadequate to house the growing number of asylum seekers, advertisements appeared in all the papers seeking suitable privately-owned accommodation.

Some hotels and other accommodation centres were purchased, others were rented. When this proved insufficient, the government bought mobile homes and placed them on government-owned sites, with electricity and sewage provided, which accommodated 1,000 asylum seekers. Prefabricated system-built homes were provided to accommodate a further 4,000. Sites of 1.5 acres or more were sought which could provide further accommodation. Accommodation was required for some 8,000 asylum seekers in 2001 alone, and accommodation was found for every single one of them.

This is not to suggest that asylum seekers are being pampered by our government while homeless people are being ignored. Indeed, in many respects, asylum seekers and refugees have a lower quality of life and less legal protections even than our own homeless people. It is simply to suggest that the plight of homeless people is not due to circumstances over which we have no control. The difference between asylum seekers who require accommodation and homeless Irish people who require accommodation is that the political will exists to solve one problem but not the other. The Minister for Justice made a decision and asylum seekers were accommodated. Homeless people still await a similar decision from the Minister for the Environment.

Some say that 'a rising tide lifts all boats'. But those who are homeless don't even have a boat. Their plight is not automatically changed with changing economic circumstances. For over a decade, Ireland experienced very difficult economic times, with very high long-term unemployment and poverty. During this period, the number of homeless, not surprisingly, increased significantly. In more recent times, with the Irish economy growing at an unprecedented pace, the rise in property values, and consequently the increase in demand for rented accommodation with a disproportionate increase in the rentals being demanded, have seen the numbers of homeless increase even further. In good times and in bad, those who are homeless continue to be homeless and their numbers continue to increase, unless decisions to remedy their plight are made by others, to whom they have no access.

Homeless people then are people who have been excluded. And so the hardest part of being homeless is not the physical discomfort, or the boredom, but living, every moment of every day, with the knowledge that you are not considered valuable, worthwhile or important enough for someone to make a decision that you should have what the rest of us take for granted, a place of your own. To be considered of so little value is to have your dignity undermined or taken away. Homeless people have to struggle to maintain their sense of their own dignity, in the face of the contrary message which their status proclaims and communicates to them on a daily, even hourly, basis.

Homeless children are particularly damaged by their homelessness. Their sense of their own identity is still being formed, their perception of themselves and of the society around them is still being moulded. To live in the knowledge that that society considers them to be nobody and does not appear to care about their homelessness is to create an adult with little or no self-respect and a lot of anger. That combination of emotions is dangerous. Is it surprising that some homeless people turn to drink or drugs to suppress their negative feelings? And that the final outcome may well be a sudden death from drugs or suicide or at best an early death from ill-health and premature old age?

Changing patterns of homelessness

Homelessness in Ireland has changed in nature over the last few years. In the first place it has increased rapidly. The Simon Community estimates that 10,000 adults are homeless in Ireland now, compared to 5,000 ten years ago. There are two broad categories of homeless people:

- those for whom poverty, combined with a crisis such as eviction or breakdown in relationship, has created a situation where the person cannot afford private housing and is not eligible, at least for a long time, for public housing
- those who have chronic personal problems.

In this second group, there are a large number of young homeless, who are drug using, and who are intimidating to the traditional, older homeless men and women for whom hostels had become their home. These older men and women move out to sleep on the streets and the hostels can no longer depend on the goodwill of volunteers to staff them but require experienced, trained and well-paid staff to cope with the difficult, disruptive behaviour of many of those who now use them. These younger, difficult homeless people have often suffered appalling traumas in their childhood, such as violence, sexual abuse, lack of love or care; some of them were introduced to drugs or alcohol by their parents at a very early age; some tried to 'parent' their parents who were often too drunk or stoned to look after themselves.

This illustrates the fact that homelessness is often not just about having nowhere to live, but also involves a multiplicity of other problems – medical, psychological, psychiatric, addiction, low self-esteem, poor relationship skills – which, if not adequately dealt with, make it impossible to maintain accommodation, even if it is made available.

Many of those in the first category above are unwilling or afraid to accept the offer of accommodation in hostels. They fear that they may find themselves sleeping next to a drug user, or be robbed of what little they have, or be offered drugs, or sexually molested. Homeless people who are not streetwise do not usually have suitable accommodation available to them, as the shortage of accommodation makes assessment of needs a pointless exercise.

In the past few years, the newly-formed Homeless Agency has tried to ensure a more co-ordinated and therefore more effective response to the plight of homeless adults. Their vision is to eliminate homelessness by the year 2010 and to minimise the risk of people becoming homeless by the provision of effective preventative policies and services. The values that have informed their plan are worth mentioning, because they are values that are often not applied by policy-makers, or even by the public, to homeless people:

- Homelessness is solvable and preventable.
- Homelessness has as much to do with social exclusion as with bricks and mortar.
- Every household is entitled to a place it can call home which is secure and appropriate to its needs and potential.
- People who become homeless are entitled to services of the highest quality.
- Each person is unique and must be valued as such.
- People who become homeless have the right to be treated with dignity and respect and to have their beliefs and choices respected.
- People who are homeless should be involved in decisions that affect them.

The Homeless Agency's plan, covering 2001–2003, is specific, detailed, comprehensive and multi-faceted. It has a total of 113 objectives covering all aspects of a homeless person's life, and includes:

- the provision of a twenty-four hour free phone service, providing advice, information and referral, targeted at people who are homeless or at risk of homelessness
- the provision of at least one hundred additional places in emergency and other hostel accommodation for street homeless people
- the provision of an additional 240 hostel places for emergency accommodation
- the provision of 200 units of transitional housing targeting a mix of families and single people in the Dublin area
- the provision of 300 additional units of long-term supported/shelter housing for single homeless people and a further 1,200 additional units of long-term housing.

For decades the problem of homelessness has been ignored. Now, under the inspired and inspiring leadership of Mary Higgins, its director, the Homeless Agency has been established and after much time, effort and consultation has produced a detailed, targeted plan which is capable of effectively solving the problem of homelessness. The test, of course, is ultimately whether its targets are met. This depends on the decisions that people make, which will determine whether homeless people have to continue living on the streets or not. Homeless people will have to wait and see. Unfortunately, it appears that the targets for the provision of accommodation sought in the three-year plan are, despite the best efforts of the Homeless Agency, hopelessly behind schedule. While this is depressing, it is hardly surprising. Homeless people have learnt from experience not to expect much.

In the past, there were two major exits out of homelessness for those who found themselves in that situation. The first was through the private rented sector. Homeless people, with financial support from the health board or the voluntary sector, paid a deposit on a flat and a weekly rent. This exit is now virtually blocked off. Due to the Celtic Tiger, many people have returned to this country and others have arrived here to seek employment and most of them seek accommodation in the private rented sector. The queues for

every vacant flat are three times longer than normal and landlords will rarely pass over a person who is working and has
the money, in order to accept a homeless person who is
unemployed and pays with a welfare cheque.

The second exit was through the local authority. But again,
this exit has been almost entirely blocked off. Due to the
Celtic Tiger, the price of property has made it impossible for
many middle-income families to afford a mortgage and so the
waiting lists for local authority accommodation have
increased dramatically. Homeless people, particularly single
homeless people, are pushed to the back of the queue with
no chance of ever seeing the key to their own front door.

Thus homeless people depend on decisions that private
landlords, managers in city councils or government ministers
make, if they are to succeed in exiting from homelessness.
However, as always in the past, there is more than a strong
possibility that homeless people will, once again, be left at
the bottom of the pile.

Homelessness and children

When we look at the problem of homeless children, we
have a very different situation. Unfortunately, the only similarity with homeless adults is that the problem of homeless
children has also been ignored by the political and social
services for decades. It was not just the failure to provide the
finances to support the services needed; there were, and
continue to be, major structural problems in the current
provision of services.

In April 2002, a heart-breaking story was revealed in the
national media. A ten-year old boy was sleeping rough. He
was so dirty that he smelled. His clothes were filthy. He had
untreated scabies. He did not go to school because the other
children laughed at him because he smelled. On some nights
he stayed with an alcoholic uncle and his alcoholic friends.
There were fears around sexual abuse. The child appeared
in the Children's Court on a Friday, summoned for non-
attendance at school. The social worker involved told the
court that the instructions she had received were *not* to take

the child into care as there were no places available for him. The judge requested the child's solicitor to bring the case, as an emergency, to the High Court that same afternoon. In the High Court, the judge ordered the health board to provide emergency care for the child over the weekend and the case would be considered in more detail on the following Monday. On the Monday, the High Court was told that an emergency foster place had been found where the child could stay until a residential place became available.

What is instructive about the above story is that emergency care *was* provided over the weekend and emergency foster care *was* provided from the Monday onwards. No doubt, obtaining this care involved considerable effort on the part of the health board; inconvenienced the social worker and some administrative staff who may have had to work late on Friday or over the weekend; and maybe some arms were twisted or pleas made or incentives offered. I don't know how it was achieved but the fact is that the care *was* provided.

Unfortunately, *the system* was unable to respond to the plight of this child. A ten-year old boy sleeping rough was unable to get the system working, a system which had statutory responsibility for dealing with situations like this. The system was unable to match the needs of this ten-year old boy to the accommodation which was available. It took an order from a High Court Judge to get some action. Emergency weekend care *was* available, foster care *was* available but the *system* couldn't find its way to providing it. While this case was newsworthy because of the age and the extreme deprivation this child was in, it nevertheless reflects a common factor in many cases of youth homelessness, namely *system failure*.

How does the system work? On the ground, homeless children access services through their local social worker. The social services are understaffed and social workers are therefore overworked. They have to prioritise. Their priorities are, rightly, very young children and children who have been, or who are alleged to have been, sexually abused. The mindset of social workers is, rightly, child protection. Hence, when a sixteen-year old, with a cigarette hanging out of his/her mouth, comes into the office to say that his/her mother has thrown him/her out of the house, it hardly ranks as a priority. The duty social worker will listen, take the details, and ask the young person to seek accommodation from the emergency, overnight, service. When the young person returns to see the duty social worker some days later, he/she will almost certainly meet a different social worker and have to tell the story all over again. Week after week, the young person returns to see the social worker and may meet different social workers on each visit. Social workers are so overworked that no-one is available to be allocated to individual young people as their own.

A young homeless person often feels like a number, not a person with a problem that someone is interested in. Many express very negative feelings about social workers. This is not the social workers' fault; they are overworked and over-stressed. Many of them do more than their best for young homeless people. But the young people need someone to give them time, to listen, to support them, to help them to deal with the crises they have been through. And time is often the one thing that social workers cannot give.

At a higher level, there are too many middle managers within the social services and there is abundant anecdotal evidence that often they do not listen to their social workers on the ground. There is a high level of frustration amongst social workers who work regularly with homeless young people. They often feel that their concerns are not being heard or adequately addressed.

At the top, there are three ministers who all may have some responsibility for homeless children. If at 9.00 am, a homeless child is arrested for shoplifting and brought to the Children's Court, that child is then the responsibility of the Minister for Justice. If the child is remanded in custody at 11.00 am, he or she becomes the responsibility of the Minister for Education. If the Juvenile Detention Centre is full and the child cannot be accepted, at 12.00 midday that child becomes the responsibility of the Minister for Health – all in the one morning! This division of responsibility leads to 'passing the buck' and young homeless people get caught in the middle with a less than adequate service.

Dealing with youth homelesness

The establishment of the Forum on Youth Homelessness in 1999, under the chairmanship of Dr Miriam Hederman O'Brien, by the former Eastern Health Board, was a serious attempt to improve the structure within which services to homeless children were delivered. The Forum produced its report in March 2000 and presented it to the Eastern Regional Health Authority, the successor to the Eastern Health Board.

The Forum was very critical of the current structures that existed to serve the needs of homeless young people. In particular, it criticised the absence of any plan to deal with the problem and the *ad-hoc* response to crises which characterised management's approach. It recommended a radically new approach – creating an independent board, a director with responsibility for the issue of homeless children, increasing the age of young homeless people whose needs are being met by these new structures from eighteen to twenty, the creation of locally-based multidisciplinary teams to work with homeless young people and the establishment of inter-linked residential placements, which would provide much greater flexibility in meeting the needs of homeless young people.

In summary, the Forum recommended:

- the designation of *one authority* to have statutory responsibility for the delivery of services to young people, aged twelve to twenty, who are out of home. (This may involve the establishment of a new executive authority.)
- the establishment of *a board* with responsibility for the effective planning, delivery and monitoring of services for young people aged between twelve and twenty out of home. It should be chaired by an independent person and have a maximum of twelve members. It should include people with relevant experience of the funding, delivery and co-ordination of services for young homeless people. It should also

include members of statutory and voluntary services, and service users. It should be the conduit for all statutory funds to the various agencies. It should have its own budget and be responsible for the discharge of its obligations

- the appointment of *a director* responsible to the board for a range of duties, including the preparation of short-term and longer-term plans, research and the co-ordination and delivery of appropriate, integrated services
- the establishment of *interlinked groups of residential units*, family placement and ancillary services. These should be flexible, localised and co-ordinated
- the designation of *(multi-disciplinary) teams*, which would include professionals from a range of different disciplines, to work with young people out of home or at risk of homelessness in the community.

Despite public assurances that all the recommendations of the Forum Report were being accepted by the Eastern Regional Health Authority, the reality is that the new structures envisaged by the Forum have, in fact, been almost completely rejected. A Director of Homelessness has been appointed but her brief is homeless adults as well as homeless children and she does not have the role or responsibilities or authority envisaged by the Forum. Multi-disciplinary teams are being created but they are not the locally-based response which the Forum considered necessary. No change in the structure of single, 'stand-alone' residential units has been proposed. The upper age remains eighteen years of age. The independent board has been flatly rejected. The same system, which has not only failed to eliminate youth homelessness over the past twenty years but has seen the problem relentlessly increase, continues to be given responsibility for dealing with the problem.

In October 2001, a Youth Homeless Strategy was published by the Department of Health and Children. It required the health boards to develop, within three months, a two-year strategic plan to eliminate youth homelessness in their areas.

The strategy was excellent. However, the data on which a comprehensive plan would be based exist only in a very inadequate, and sometimes inaccurate, form. Data in relation to the numbers of homeless children, the areas they come from and their needs, are in short supply. It was difficult to see how a comprehensive and detailed plan could have been produced. However, the Youth Homeless Strategy was the first attempt to seriously deal with the problem. It sought to eliminate youth homelessness within two years. It demanded that the health boards produce their plans to do so. Homeless children, like homeless adults, must wait and see.

The role of government

The common good takes precedence over private, vested interests. It is the role of government to promote the common good and to ensure its priority over private interests. That people should have a place that they can call home is a right that most of us take for granted. We would find it intolerable that we should be left to sleep on the street. But when those who are appointed or elected to promote the common good find that private interests are in conflict with the decisions which the common good require, then people will be left excluded.

In 1973, the Kenny report on land in urban areas recommended that all land zoned for development in the vicinity of urban areas should be purchased by the local authority at its current value plus twenty-five per cent. The local authority could then utilise the land in the interests of the common good. Although the report was chaired by a High Court Judge, the government of the day decided that such a recommendation would be unconstitutional. In hindsight, it is clear that such a recommendation conflicted with the private interests of those in government and their friends in the construction industry. The result is that today accommodation for those on low incomes is very scarce and people remain homeless.

Apart from the right to life, which is in a category all of its own, the fundamental human rights are: the right to adequate food, the right to a basic education, the right to a place called home, the right to basic health care and the right to work. Each of these rights is denied to some people in Irish society – they are excluded from the very fabric of society. A just society is one which ensures that citizens have their fundamental rights guaranteed by law and provided through the structures of the state, which seeks to ensure that the private, vested interests of individuals cannot obstruct the fundamental rights of others. In the Ireland of the Celtic Tiger, some are unfortunately going in the opposite direction.

Whither the Arts Council?*

Patricia Quinn

Introduction

Having grown and prospered in its first half-century, the Arts Council is now entering a period of enormous change. The implementation of the second Arts Plan (completed in 2001), the launch of the third Arts Plan 2002-2006, and, most importantly, the publication of revising arts legislation in Spring 2002 raise the question of what is in store for the Council as it enters its second half-century. A number of themes emerge from a brief survey of the Council's role as an instrument of public provision for the arts, and they point to a re-definition of the Arts Council's role *vis-à-vis* that of central government on the one hand, and local government on the other. How effectively the Council negotiates its changing role in these relationships will contribute to its success in the future. One thing is clear: despite the changing and more crowded arts policy environment, the Arts Council must retain its autonomy in order to remain effective.

A half-century of activity

In 2001, the Arts Council celebrated its fiftieth anniversary, and in early 2002 the Minister for Arts Heritage, Gaeltacht and the Islands published a third Arts Bill, signalling government's intention to give the institution a further lease of life. Thus, it is timely to look at how the Council has served the public in its first half-century, and how it should continue to do so over the next fifty years.

---

* It has not been possible to incorporate several developments that have taken place since this chapter was written in summer 2002.

The new Bill marks for the first time in arts legislation the presence in cabinet of a minister with responsibility for the arts. As might be expected, it goes further, and defines a role for the minister in determining arts policy. This impacts very directly on the Arts Council which, until now, has had the freedom not only to set its own priorities but to determine its own agenda.

When it was founded in November 1951, the Arts Council was consciously styled after the model that had already been established under the chairmanship of John Maynard Keynes in post-War Britain: a government-appointed arms' length body, with the remit to promote, support and assist the arts in Ireland. Similar bodies were established throughout the colonies and former colonies of Britain, and in Northern Europe, and indeed so robust is the model that new variants on it are being developed in Africa, in south-east Asia, and in post-Communist Eastern Europe to this day.

In general, in the larger European countries, Ministries of Culture provide support to the major national cultural institutions, and their work is augmented at regional and city levels by culture departments within regional or local government. By contrast, in the United States, whereas state and city Arts Councils and the National Endowment for the Arts provide locally and nationally for the arts, public support is greatly exceeded by private giving on the part of individuals (with the benefit of tax incentives) and of the many foundations endowed in the name of their wealthy benefactors.

Brian P. Kennedy's excellent history of the Irish Arts Council from its foundation until 1989[1] provides an insight into the vision of its godparents, Thomas Bodkin (former Director of the National Gallery) and Paddy Little (Minister for Posts & Telegraphs in the Fianna Fáil government of 1944-1948, and the Council's first Director 1951-1956), and the motivation of its political sponsors from all parts of the political spectrum.

The sponsors of the Arts Council idea had worthy, if rather generally-expressed aims. While a number of ambitious capital cultural projects fell by the wayside in successive administrations during the second half of the 1940s (including one plan to purchase the lease of the Rotunda buildings for a national concert hall, and another to relocate the National Library to the then site of the Fitzwilliam Lawn Tennis Club), the decade saw intensive efforts to improve public provision for the contemporary arts.

The proposals for the creation of the Arts Council survived the change of government of June 1951. Eamon de Valera's government acted swiftly to follow through on the Bill enacted in the last month of John A. Costello's outgoing inter-party administration. Both men spoke in high rhetorical terms of the importance of this new institution. De Valera told the members of the first Arts Council that their task was 'to give our people an abiding interest in the intellectual life and to stimulate them to aspire to win for our nation a worthy place in the realms of culture ...'.[2] 'There will be no nationality without art,' said John A. Costello. 'It is the duty of every Irish government to give every help to the arts and the application of art to industry.'[3]

In practice, the Council enjoyed considerable freedom to interpret its mandate from successive governments. Following Paddy Little's retirement, Seán O'Faoláin, appointed in late 1956 despite the express opposition of the Catholic Archbishop of Dublin, Dr John Charles McQuaid, brought the Council through some precedent-setting conflicts of principle with government, which helped set a style of independence and standard of autonomy in artistic decision-making that were to serve the Council repeatedly, if not always consistently, in subsequent years.

This autonomy was not exercised to any very controversial purpose in the Council's first two decades. Following the collapse of Paddy Little's ambitious vision of a national organisation supported by local advisory committees in 10 regional centres (including Dublin), the Dublin-based Council soon settled into a rhythm of supporting a relatively narrow range of artistic activities, especially in the visual arts. The Council was a major patron of the work of visual artists, and purchased their work for loaning out to public buildings, or for show in directly-promoted exhibitions. It also organised public lectures, and provided guarantees against loss to a small number of musical and dramatic productions.

In the 1960s, the Council turned its back on a Europe-wide trend in democratising access to the arts and broadening definitions of the role of the State in supporting them. In a key change to its Standing Orders, the Council changed the existing remit, agreed in 1957, that 'the future policy, while not failing to encourage local enterprise, would insist on high standards' to read: 'The Council's main function is to maintain and encourage high standards in the arts.' Anything judged to fall outside the category of 'fine or applied arts' was therefore explicitly excluded – a narrow interpretation of the mandate of the Council under the 1951 Arts Act.

Following a period of growing criticism of the Arts Council for its perceived conservatism and narrowness of perspective, a second Arts Act introduced by the Fine Gael/Labour coalition of 1973 amended the first. Critics included Charles Haughey TD who, as Minister for Finance in the late 1960s, had tried (and failed) to promote the idea of root and branch structural reform of the Council. Despite his disappointment at the limited ambition of the second Act, he commented: 'the implementation of an enlightened comprehensive policy for the Arts with adequate financial provision enshrined in it [is] an essential part – I use the word essential deliberately – of modern progressive government.'[4] In the Senate, Mary Robinson was another critic, suggesting that the Arts Council had failed to be responsive or accountable, and questioning whether new legislation would really improve this situation.[5]

In this context, an enlarged Arts Council took office on 31 December 1973 with a sense of having something to prove. It had 17 members, and their selection, as required under the new Act, had specific regard for their 'attainments or interest in or ... knowledge of the arts, or ... competence otherwise to assist the Council', and for the need to secure 'a balanced representation as between branches of the arts'[6] – a matter on which the first Act had been silent.

The new Council, whose members included prominent practising artists like Séamus Heaney, John B. Keane, Hugh Maguire and Andrew Devane, moved to enlarge the field of the Council's interests and concerns, in a number of ways. It introduced new direct supports for individual artists, and looked for ways of stimulating local authorities to exploit the new powers given to them in the 1973 Act to '... assist with money or in kind or by the provision of services or facilities which ... would, in the opinion of the authority, stimulate public interest in the arts, promote the knowledge, appreciation and practice of the arts ...'[7] It welcomed the hand-over of funding responsibility from other agencies for five prominent cultural institutions (The Abbey and Gate Theatre Companies, the Irish Theatre Company, the Irish Ballet Company and the Dublin Theatre Festival) and augmented its professional staff following the appointment of Colm Ó Briain as Director.

It would be wrong however to characterise this time in the Arts Council's history as one simply of enlargement or aggrandisement. In these years, the Council forged an identity as a values-driven organisation, publicly advocating the significance of the arts, and seeking to influence the policy agenda outside of its own immediate remit – in particular in provision for the arts in education. It commissioned a number of important reports,[8] and enlarged the field of its policy concerns, for example by beginning to provide support to contemporary dance and film.

In discussing the circumstances in which the reforming legislation of 1973 was framed and adopted, Brian Kennedy asks[9] whether a fundamental shift had occurred in official thinking about state patronage of the arts. Would the government treat cultural development the same way it had treated economic development by publishing a five-year plan with set targets? Kennedy's answer to his own question is no. In fact, as he points out, the question was never even considered by government.

In 1984, following the appointment of Adrian Munnelly as the new Director, the Council consolidated its relatively piecemeal local arts development initiatives and undertook a concerted effort to exploit to the full the enlargement of local government's powers provided for in the '73 Act. It entered into agreements with local authorities throughout the country for the appointment of local arts development officers. It helped build up the local infrastructure for the arts – in the main, by providing grants to assist the development of theatres and arts centres in major urban centres: Cork, Limerick, Sligo, Waterford, Wexford. It supplemented this emergent human and physical infrastructure with increased touring grants to theatre, opera and dance productions, with a new organisation to improve local concert promotion, and a series of touring exhibitions. It also supported major new multi-disciplinary festivals in Galway, Kilkenny, Sligo and elsewhere, seeing them as among the most effective means of broadening public participation in the arts.

Perhaps inevitably, as the Arts Council proliferated its policy and funding interests, its financial resources began to lag far behind the accelerating demands from artists and newly-developing arts organisations. Funding from government (the Council's only source of revenue) did not grow in the 1980s in line with the needs of its expanding client base and an increasingly articulate arts sector – which the Arts Council very much saw itself as representing. 'There is a crisis in the arts,' declared the eighth Council, seeking recognition for the greater breadth of the sector and its needs, and pointing to the growing professionalisation of artistic practice and management on the one hand, and, on the other, the findings of an important report[10] on the need for concerted efforts on the part of the Council and others to enhance audiences.

However, at the end of the 1980s, with the appointment of the ninth Arts Council in 1988, notwithstanding the continuing low levels of arts funding (relative both to demand from artists and arts organisations, and to public provision elsewhere in developed countries), the Council began to move away from a posture of public confrontation with government, and to explore other means of lobbying for recognition of the needs of the arts. In 1993, for example, the Council augmented its annual bids for grant-in-aid with a report to government on the medium-term capital development needs of the arts nationally.[11] The call to consolidate provision for the arts with capital investment by government can be seen as the turning point when the 'hand to mouth' dispensation under which the arts resided for so long began to come to an end.

In January 1993, the Fianna Fáil/Labour coalition government created for the first time a full cabinet post with responsibility for the arts and culture, augmenting the existing role of the Minister for the Gaeltacht to create the Department for Arts, Culture and the Gaeltacht. Elements of the new Department were drawn from a variety of sources, including the Departments of the Taoiseach (arts, culture), Transport, Energy and Communications (radio and broadcasting), and the Office of Public Works (heritage policy). The first Minister to hold the title, Michael D. Higgins TD, introduced two significant innovations: he asked for, and received, the first-ever published strategy plan from the Council in 1994 – the Arts Plan 1995-1998.

The statement of remit published by the Council in that first plan gave an indication of how far it had moved from the dominant and narrowly-defined preoccupation with artistic excellence specified in the 1960s. 'As the statutory body entrusted with stimulating public interest in the arts and with promoting knowledge, appreciation and practice of the arts, An Chomhairle Ealaíon/the Arts Council believes that everyone in Ireland has an entitlement to meaningful access to and participation in the arts.' Significantly, in this first and in subsequent plans, the Council identified partnership with others – especially local authorities – as a critical means of realising its purpose.

In 1995, Minister Higgins announced a major capital programme for the arts – the Cultural Development Incentive Scheme, co-funded by the Exchequer and the European Regional Development Fund (ERDF). Although not the first capital programme for the arts to be provided by government (funding for the development of Temple Bar as a cultural quarter had been provided under the Urban Renewal Programme of the ERDF the previous year), this scheme articulated for the first time government recognition of – and moreover the will to provide resources for – the needs of artists and the demand from the public for permanent facilities throughout Ireland for making, rehearsing, producing, exhibiting and performing art. (The fund also provided for local museums and other heritage facilities.)

The requirement for matching funding from local authorities acted as a major stimulus to the arts agenda within local government. The fact that this was a limited fund for which local authorities could tender competitively drove a local input to cultural policy that had been absent from previous government capital investment in the arts – principally major once-off investments in the 1980s in institutions like the National Concert Hall and the Royal Hospital Kilmainham, later the home of the Irish Museum of Modern Art.

Síle de Valera TD, the second incumbent of the office of Minister (the title of the Department was changed to Arts, Heritage, Gaeltacht and the Islands), followed this pattern; she secured full funding for the first plan, asked the Council for a second and subsequently for a third Arts Plan, and secured a further round of capital funds to augment recently-developed new venues in established or emerging urban centres in Portlaoise, Mullingar, Letterkenny, Galway, Cork, Tallaght, Dún Laoghaire, Blanchardstown and elsewhere.

It is fair to say that the cultural map of Ireland has been transformed since the State first chose to legislate for the needs of the arts in 1951. Successive governments have grown the levels of financial commitment, New legislation[12] has been proposed that aims to express the role of the Minister in policy terms, while at the same time re-affirming the concept of the Arts Council's autonomy in decision-making – a feature of public provision for the arts for the last 50 years. Thus, for the time being at least, Irish public policy identifies the arts as a central concern of government, but also recognises a distinction between state control and state support for the arts.

A changing policy environment

But while this central principle has remained, many other changes have come about in the public policy environment for the arts. For a start, the Arts Council is no longer the only player. At central government level, the determination for the first time in the history of the state to invest significantly in rolling programmes of support for arts infrastructure throughout the country augurs a new level of recognition for the value of the arts in people's lives.

Equally important, the government's engagement with the Arts Council's work has become more active, driven by the production and adoption of arts plans whose implementation has become government policy, expressed in the form of successive programmes for government. The effect of reforms in public governance generally has been to transform the operating environment of the Arts Council, introducing a level of transparency and accountability in its operations that were unimagined when arts legislation was last reviewed in 1973.

Local government bodies have not only developed significant and increasingly sophisticated arts policy and planning provision through the adoption of arts plans and the employment of arts staff, they have been mandated under the Local Government Act to produce Social, Cultural and Economic development strategies. In their very title, these strategies recognise the centrality of culture in influencing the quality of people's lives. Local government's involvement in joint-funding the development of new buildings for the arts has followed through in a more active engagement with the operation of these venues, and they have become very significant funders of the work of visual artists in particular through their use of 'percent for art' as a mechanism to commission major work of public art.

Other public agencies are recognising that the arts play a role in their strategies, and bodies like Údarás na Gaeltachta, Bord Fáilte and the Eastern Regional Health Authority have undertaken research and development work in cooperation with the Arts Council to improve their capability to provide effectively for the arts as a dimension of their work.

It follows that in this changing – and more crowded – policy environment, the Arts Council must look to its particular value-adding role, to ask what are the things that it uniquely does, and look to how these are to be done in the future. The Council's latest reiteration of its remit explicitly

recognises that things have changed: '... We work in the context of a public policy that aims to enable the people of
Ireland to express as participants or engage as audiences
with their own and others' cultures.'[13] The Council has proposed, and Government has agreed, that the requirements of
the arts now demand a different kind of organisation, specifically charged with developing as well as funding the arts
in Ireland. The kind of areas where non-grant supports are
needed even more than grants include the international dimension of the arts, the arts in education, and the development
of better management and governance in arts organisations.

Delivering these kinds of developmental services requires a
degree of organisation reform, not just of the non-executive
structure as specified in the Bill, but within the Council's
staff. This reform is overdue and pressing. The professional
bureaucracy first created in the mid-1970s, and changed very
little since then, needs to be overhauled comprehensively to
deal with the challenges of a very different set of demands
– whether from the public and an increasingly profession-
alised arts sector, or from government at national or local
levels. The issues of organisation design and capacity are not
exclusive to the Arts Council,[14] but they have been variously
identified in the independent evaluations of both the first
and second Arts Plans[15] as critical to the Council's capacity
to think and act in a genuinely strategic way.

Finally, and perhaps paradoxically, the promise of more
highly articulated government cultural policy, and the presence of published arts planning strategies, for all that they
bring greater clarity and accountability to the work of the
Arts Council (or at least the promise of these good things)
should not create some kind of reductionist strait-jacket
confining the future role of the Arts Council solely to that of
delivering fixed-term service level agreements to the
Government.

The conditions of uncertainty and embryonic recognition
of the needs of the arts created enormous constraints for the
Arts Council in terms of what it could aspire to or achieve
during its first half-century. Nevertheless, the culture of the
organisation that emerged is committed to advocating

the fundamental and intrinsic values of the arts. That is the legacy of the dozens of citizens – artists and otherwise – who have served on its board. As the Council rebuilds its institutional premises within the scaffolding of the changed statutory framework, it will surely restate the benefits of its continued autonomy to the further development of the arts in Ireland.

Notes

1 Brian P. Kennedy, *Dreams and Responsibilities* (The Arts Council 1990)

2 Kennedy, *op. cit.*, p. 100

3 Ibid.

4 *Dáil Debates*, Vol. 268, 17 Oct. 1973, cols. 62-3

5 *Seanad Debates*, Vol. 76, 14 Nov. 1973, col. 15

6 Kennedy, *op. cit.*, p. 166

7 The Arts Act, 1973

8 *The Place of the Arts in Irish Education.* Report of the Arts Council's Working Party on the Arts in Education. Ciarán Benson. Dublin, 1979.

9 Kennedy, *op. cit.*, p. 166

10 *Audiences, Acquisitions and Amateurs.* Dublin, 1983

11 *A Capital Programme for the Arts* (1993)

12 At the time of writing in July 2002, the Arts Bill 2001 is at its Second Stage.

13 The Arts Plan 2002-2006

14 They have been developed with considerable insight by John Murray in his paper *Reflections on the SMI* (TCD Policy Institute Working Papers November 2001)

15 Indecon/PriceWaterhouse Coopers, *Succeeding Better: Report of the Strategic Review of the Arts Plan 1995-1998* (Government Publications November 1998); Anthony Everitt, *Evaluation of the Arts Plan 1999-2001* (The Arts Council July 2001)